Update

VERONA

Tourist Guide 2024

Unveiling The Complete Travel Companion For a Journey of History and Culture in Italy's City of Love, With Insider Tips, Top Attractions and Timeless Adventures

Anya Silver

Acknowledgement and Disclaimer

We have dedicated significant effort to ensure that this travel guide provides accurate and up-to-date information as of its publication date. However, we recognize that certain details such as contact information, operating hours, pricing, and travel details may be subject to change. We cannot be held responsible for any inconvenience that may arise from using this guide or for the accuracy and suitability of information sourced from third parties.

We strongly encourage readers to independently verify the information presented in this guide and to confirm any specifics with the relevant establishments or authorities before concluding travel plans. Please stay vigilant for any updates or changes that may occur after the publication of this guide.

Your safety and satisfaction are our top priorities, and we sincerely appreciate your understanding of the dynamic nature of travel-related information. We hope that this guide enhances your journey and serves as a valuable resource throughout your travels.

Table Of Contents

INTRODUCTION: WELCOME TO VERONA

Welcome to the enchanting world of Verona, where history, culture, and timeless romance weave together in a tapestry of unforgettable experiences. In this updated Verona Tourist Guide, we invite you to embark on a journey through this splendid city, discovering its hidden treasures, rich traditions, and vibrant modern life.

As you hold this guide in your hands, envision yourself strolling through Verona's charming streets, savoring delectable cuisine, and basking in the warm Italian sun. This is not just another travel guide; it's your golden key to an authentic Veronese adventure.

In the bustling world of travel literature, what sets this guide apart? It's not just about listing places to visit, but about immersing you in the soul of Verona. This guide is more than pages, it was crafted with passion and a sprinkle of firsthand experiences. it's a promise of remarkable experiences and priceless memories.

My own visit to Verona was a revelation of the city's hidden gems and vibrant culture. Each cobblestone street seemed to whisper secrets of Verona's storied past, and every local dish I savored brought a taste of authentic Italian life. This guide is not just the result of research; it's a testament to the passion I felt while exploring this remarkable city.

Over the years, I've come to know Verona intimately. From the grandeur of the Verona Arena to the quaint charm of Juliet's House, each visit has been a revelation. And now, through these pages, I'm passing on the wisdom gained from those journeys to you.

So, are you ready to create your own Verona story? With this guide, you'll embark on an adventure that will leave you breathless, awestruck, and eager for more. Dive in, and let Verona cast its spell on you.

Experience Verona like a true traveler, not just a tourist, and let this "Updated VERONA Tourist Guide" be your trusted companion, your confidante and your guide through the treasures of this magnificent city.

Unveiling Verona - A Brief Overview

History

Nestled along the winding Adige River, Verona is a city that breathes history. Its roots stretch back over two millennia, bearing witness to the rise and fall of empires, and the tapestry of cultures that have left their mark.

Founded by the ancient Romans in the 1st century BC, Verona thrived as a key hub along the Via Claudia Augusta, a major trade route. It became a pivotal Roman colony known as "Verona Augusta," renowned for its strategic importance and thriving commerce.

In the following centuries, Verona witnessed the shifting tides of power. It fell under the sway of various empires, including the Ostrogoths and the Lombards, before being integrated into the powerful Venetian Republic in the late

Middle Ages. The city's architecture still bears the influences of these diverse rulers.

The Renaissance brought a renewed cultural and artistic fervor to Verona, with the city becoming a flourishing center of learning and the arts. This era gifted Verona with architectural marvels like the Palazzo della Ragione and the stunning Teatro Filarmonico.

Verona's history also echoes with the footsteps of Shakespeare's star-crossed lovers, Romeo and Juliet. While the tale is fictional, Juliet's House, with its iconic balcony, has become an enduring symbol of romanticism.

Today, Verona stands as a living testament to its rich past. Its streets are a living museum, where ancient Roman ruins coexist with medieval palaces and Renaissance treasures. Each stone, each archway, carries with it the whispers of centuries gone by.

Culture

Verona is a city in northeastern Italy with a rich and vibrant culture. Its tapestry of Roman, medieval, and Renaissance influences creates a captivating backdrop for exploration. It is home to a number of important historical and cultural sites, including the Roman Arena, Juliet's House, and Castel Vecchio. Verona is also known for its opera, its food and wine, and its lively atmosphere.

- **Architectural Marvels:** Verona's skyline is a testament to its diverse heritage. Roman structures like the Verona Arena stand alongside Gothic masterpieces like the Basilica di San Zeno, showcasing a spectrum of architectural styles.

- **Shakespearean Legacy:** Verona's association with Shakespeare's "Romeo and Juliet" is etched in its identity. Juliet's House, with its iconic balcony, draws starry-eyed visitors. The city's romantic aura is palpable, making it a perennial favorite for lovers.

- **Opera Extravaganza:** The Verona Arena, a nearly 2,000-year-old Roman amphitheater, hosts one of the world's most renowned opera festivals. The grandeur of this historic venue elevates performances to a transcendent level.

- **Culinary Delights:** Verona's gastronomy is a symphony of flavors. Indulge in local specialties like risotto all'Amarone and delectable Amarone wine. Osterias and trattorias offer a taste of authentic Veronese cuisine.

- **Festivals and Traditions:** Verona's calendar is punctuated with lively festivals. Vinitaly, a prestigious wine fair, showcases the region's viticultural prowess. The Carnival of Verona and the Feast of San Zeno provide immersive cultural experiences.

Warm Hospitality: Veronese locals are known for their warmth and friendliness. Engage with them to unearth hidden gems and gain a deeper understanding of the city's customs.

- **Language:** While Italian is the official language, locals often infuse conversations with Veronese dialect, showcasing their regional pride.

Geographical Location

Situated in the Veneto region of northern Italy, Verona graces the banks of the Adige River, a picturesque setting against the backdrop of the Lessini Mountains to the north and the Po Valley to the south. Its strategic location places it in close proximity to other Italian gems like Venice and Milan, making it an accessible and ideal hub for exploration.

Verona's coordinates, approximately 45.4384° N latitude and 10.9916° E longitude, position it as a gateway to the stunning landscapes of the Veneto region. This city's beauty is not confined to its historic center; the surrounding countryside offers rolling hills adorned with vineyards, providing a scenic contrast to its urban core.

When exploring Verona, its geographical context provides a deeper appreciation for its varied landscapes and the influences that have shaped its cultural and historical tapestry. As you navigate its streets and take in its vistas, you'll find yourself enchanted by the harmonious dance between nature and human history that defines this captivating city.

Climate and Timezone

Verona has a humid subtropical climate, with warm, humid summers and mild, wet winters. The average temperature in July is 24°C (75°F), and the average temperature in January is 4°C (39°F). It is a good time to visit Verona year-round, but the best time to visit is during the spring (April-May) or fall (September-October), when the weather is mild and there are fewer crowds.

Verona, like the rest of Italy, operates in the Central European Time (CET) zone. When Daylight Saving Time is in effect, it follows Central European Summer

Time (CEST). This means Verona is typically 1 hour ahead of Greenwich Mean Time (GMT+1) during standard time and 2 hours ahead (GMT+2) during Daylight Saving Time.

Being aware of the timezone is crucial for planning activities, making reservations, and catching trains or flights, ensuring you make the most of your time in this captivating city.

Why Choose Verona for Your Vacation?

When it comes to choosing a destination for your vacation, Verona stands tall among the crowd. Here's why this ancient Italian city should be at the top of your list:

1. A Tapestry of History and Romance: Verona's cobbled streets are imbued with centuries of history, and it's very air seems to resonate with whispers of love stories immortalized by Shakespeare. From Juliet's iconic balcony to the imposing Castelvecchio, every corner of Verona tells a tale of a bygone era.

2. The Veronese Culinary Symphony: For any traveler with a penchant for culinary delights, Verona is a feast for the senses. Picture yourself savoring al dente pasta with a glass of local Amarone wine, or indulging in creamy gelato under the Italian sun. Verona's gastronomic offerings are nothing short of a symphony of flavors.

3. A City of Timeless Elegance: Verona's architecture is a testament to the city's enduring elegance. Roman ruins, medieval castles, and Renaissance palaces coexist seamlessly, creating a visual marvel at every turn. The Verona Arena, a Roman amphitheater that has withstood the test of time, stands as a proud sentinel to the city's grandeur.

4. The Warm Embrace of Local Hospitality: Veronese locals exude a warmth and friendliness that can transform a mere visit into a heartwarming experience.

Whether you're seeking recommendations for the best trattoria or simply engaging in casual conversation in a café, you'll find the people of Verona ever-ready with a smile.

5. Gateway to the Enchanting Veneto Region: Verona's strategic location offers access to the wonders of the Veneto region. From the serene beauty of Lake Garda to the architectural marvels of Vicenza, day trips from Verona promise adventures beyond the city limits.

6. Every Season, a Different Verona: Verona's charm transcends the seasons. Whether you're basking in the summer sun amidst blooming gardens or wandering through cozy, mist-kissed streets in winter, Verona wears its beauty in every season.

7. A City of Festivals and Celebrations: Verona knows how to celebrate life. From the world-renowned Opera Festival at the Arena to local wine festivals, Verona's calendar is peppered with events that promise unforgettable experiences.

8. Affordability: Verona is a relatively affordable city to visit, especially compared to other major Italian cities, such as Rome and Venice. There are a number of budget-friendly hotels and restaurants in Verona, and the city has a good public transportation system.

Best Times to Visit Verona

As a seasoned visitor to Verona, I've come to appreciate that the city's charm shimmers in every season. Here are some insider tips on the best times to visit this enchanting destination:

1. Spring (March to May): Springtime in Verona is a symphony of blossoms and mild temperatures. The city awakens from its winter slumber, offering a perfect blend of pleasant weather and fewer crowds. Don't miss the chance to explore the blooming gardens and enjoy outdoor activities.

2. Summer (June to August): The summer months are bustling with life and energy in Verona. The warm weather invites outdoor exploration, and the city comes alive with festivals and events. To beat the crowds, aim for early morning or late evening visits to popular attractions.

3. Autumn (September to November): Autumn brings a magical transformation to Verona, painting it in a tapestry of golden hues. The weather is still inviting, and the city is adorned with a romantic ambiance. Take leisurely strolls through parks and enjoy the rich colors of the season.

4. Winter (December to February): Verona in winter has a special kind of charm. While the temperatures dip, the city exudes a cozy atmosphere, especially around the holiday season. Visit the Christmas markets for unique gifts and warm up with a cup of Italian hot chocolate.

While the summer Opera Festival at the Verona Arena is a must-see, consider attending a performance in early September. The weather is still pleasant, and the crowds have slightly diminished, allowing for a more intimate experience.

What to Pack - Packing Smart

Here's a guide on what to pack to ensure you're prepared for every enchanting moment in this historic city:

1. Comfortable Footwear: Verona's cobblestone streets are charming but can be unforgiving on your feet. Opt for comfortable walking shoes or sneakers to explore the city comfortably.

2. Light Layers: Verona's climate can be unpredictable. Pack versatile clothing like breathable fabrics, light sweaters, and a waterproof jacket to adapt to changing weather.

3. Modest Attire for Visiting Churches: If you plan to visit churches like the Basilica di San Zeno, ensure you have clothing that covers shoulders and knees as a sign of respect.

4. Adapters and Chargers: European plug types (Type C and Type F) are used in Verona. Don't forget to bring adapters for your electronic devices and chargers to keep them powered up.

5. Reusable Water Bottle: Staying hydrated while exploring Verona is essential. Bring a reusable water bottle to refill throughout the day, especially during warmer months.

6. Sun Protection: Sunglasses, a wide-brimmed hat, and sunscreen are essential, especially in the summer. Verona's sunny days can be intense, and it's important to protect yourself from UV rays.

7. Travel Guide and Maps: Good thing you have this travel guide, while digital resources are handy, a physical travel guide and a city map can be invaluable. They provide a tangible reference and don't rely on battery life.

8. Compact Umbrella: Verona is known for occasional rain showers, even in the warmer months. A compact umbrella can be a lifesaver when unexpected weather strikes.

9. Daypack or Crossbody Bag: A small, comfortable bag for daily excursions will help keep your essentials organized and easily accessible.

10. Travel Insurance and Important Documents: Ensure you have copies of your passport, travel insurance, hotel reservations, and any necessary travel documents stored securely.

11. Personal Medications and First Aid Kit: Bring any prescription medications you require, along with a basic first aid kit for minor emergencies.

By packing smart and considering the specific needs of your Verona adventure, you'll be well-prepared to soak in every moment of this captivating city. Remember to leave some space in your luggage for the souvenirs and cherished memories you'll bring back home. Happy travels

Extra Tips

● Bring a carry-on bag: This will ensure that you have everything you need in case your luggage is lost or delayed.

● Roll your clothes instead of folding them: Rolling your clothes will save space in your suitcase.

Random Facts About Verona

1. Verona is known as the "City of Love" because it is the setting for Shakespeare's Romeo and Juliet.

2. The Roman Arena in Verona is one of the best-preserved Roman amphitheaters in the world.

3. Verona is home to the world's oldest opera festival, the Arena di Verona Opera Festival.

4. Verona is also known for its delicious food and wine, including Amarone and Valpolicella wines.

5. Verona is a popular tourist destination, but it is also a great place to live and work.

6. Verona is home to a number of universities and colleges, making it a vibrant and youthful city.

7. Verona is also a major transportation hub, with direct train connections to major Italian cities, such as Rome, Milan, and Florence.

8. Verona is a relatively affordable city to live in, especially compared to other major Italian cities, such as Rome and Venice.

9. Verona is a popular destination for expats, due to its affordable cost of living, high quality of life, and proximity to other major European cities.

10. Verona is a great place to raise a family, with a number of good schools and plenty of family-friendly activities.

11. Verona is also a great place to retire, with a mild climate and a number of amenities for seniors.

12. The Scaligeri family, known for their iconic tomb structures, ruled Verona in the 13th and 14th centuries. Their rule left a lasting mark on the city's architecture and history.

13. Verona hosts the annual Brà-Bra Festival, an artistic event where hundreds of volunteers help to create a colossal bra, symbolizing unity and breast cancer awareness.

14. Ponte Pietra, Verona's oldest bridge, has an intriguing history. Initially constructed by the Romans, it was rebuilt in the 14th century after being destroyed by an earthquake.

15. The nearby town of Soave is celebrated for its eponymous wine, a crisp and refreshing white variety produced from the Garganega grape.

What NOT To Do In Verona

Having visited Verona on several occasions for years, I've learned a thing or two about navigating this city. Here are some insider tips on what to avoid during your visit:

1. Skipping the Side Streets: Don't limit yourself to the main thoroughfares. Some of the most charming spots in Verona are found in its hidden alleyways. Take the time to explore and you'll be rewarded with delightful surprises.

2. Overlooking Local Eateries: Avoid sticking solely to tourist-heavy restaurants. Seek out local osterias and trattorias for an authentic taste of Veronese cuisine. These hidden gems often offer a more genuine experience.

3. Ignoring the Riverbanks: Don't forget to stroll along the Adige River. The views of the city from Ponte Pietra are breathtaking, and the riverbanks offer a tranquil escape from the city's hustle and bustle.

4. Neglecting the Local Dialect: Veronese locals often speak a unique dialect. While many are fluent in Italian, attempting a few phrases in the local dialect (like "Siora" for "Signora" or "Sior" for "Signor") can earn you a warm smile.

5. Disregarding Historical Context: Don't rush through the historic sites without soaking in their history. Take a moment to appreciate the architectural details and imagine the stories that unfolded within these ancient walls.

6. Neglecting Reservations for Opera Performances: If you plan to attend an opera at the Verona Arena, don't assume you can purchase tickets on the spot. These performances are incredibly popular and often sell out, so it's wise to book in advance.

7. Avoiding Day Trips: While Verona has much to offer, don't limit yourself to just the city. Day trips to nearby destinations like Lake Garda, Soave, and Vicenza unveil even more of the Veneto region's treasures.

8. Disregarding Local Customs: Veronese people value politeness and respect for traditions. Remember to greet locals with a friendly "Buongiorno" or "Buonasera" and show appreciation for their culture.

9. Overpacking: Resist the urge to bring your entire wardrobe. Verona's relaxed atmosphere means you can get away with packing light, leaving room for the souvenirs and keepsakes you'll want to bring back.

10. Rushing Through Juliet's House: While Juliet's House is a must-see, don't rush through it. Take a moment on the balcony, soak in the courtyard, and appreciate the love notes left by visitors from around the world. Don't skip the line as this is one of Verona's most popular tourist attractions, the line can get very long. However, it is definitely worth the wait.

11. Don't wear high heels: Verona is a very walkable city, so be sure to wear comfortable shoes. High heels are not recommended, as you will be doing a lot of walking.

12. Don't be afraid to get lost: Verona is a relatively small city, so it is easy to get around. Should you find yourself in unfamiliar territory, don't hesitate to approach a resident and request guidance. Veronese people are generally very friendly and helpful.

By avoiding these common pitfalls, you'll be able to immerse yourself more deeply in the Veronese experience and uncover the city's true magic.

Here are some additional tips for avoiding common tourist traps in Verona:

● Be careful of people selling souvenirs: Some people selling souvenirs may try to overcharge you. Make sure to haggle for a better price before paying for the item.

- Be careful of restaurants with menus in multiple languages: Restaurants with menus in multiple languages are often tourist traps. The food is often overpriced and the quality is not very good.

- Be careful of taxis: Some taxi drivers may try to overcharge tourists. It is advisable to discuss and agree upon the taxi fare with the driver prior to entering the vehicle.

- Be careful of pickpockets: Pickpocketing is a problem in many tourist destinations, including Verona. Take care of your valuables and be mindful of your surroundings.

Visa Requirements

Understanding the visa requirements is an essential step in ensuring a smooth and hassle-free entry into this enchanting city.

Visa requirements to enter Verona, Italy vary depending on your nationality. Citizens of most European Union

(EU) and Schengen Area countries do not need a visa to enter Italy for stays of up to 90 days (3 months) within a 180-day period (6 months). You can check online or the Italian consulate in your home country if your country is included as the list is exhaustive.

However, of your country is included such as United States, UK and Schengen countries you will need to bring the following documents with you:

- A valid passport or national identity card.
- Proof of health insurance.
- Proof of sufficient funds to support yourself for the duration of your stay.
- A return ticket or proof of onward travel.
- You may also be asked to show proof of accommodation, but this is not always required.

If you are planning to stay in Verona for longer than 90 days, before you leave your home country, you will need to apply for a long-stay visa. You have the option to complete this process at the Italian embassy or consulate located in your country of residence.

If your country is not included then you will need to apply for a visa to enter Italy. Visa applications can be made at the Italian embassy or consulate in your home country.

Documents Needed for Visa Application:

1. A Completed Visa Application Form: Obtain the official visa application form from the Italian consulate or embassy in your home country. Please ensure that all provided information is both precise and current.

2. Valid Passport: Make sure that your passport is valid for at least six months beyond your intended date of departure from the Schengen Area. The passport must additionally contain a minimum of two empty pages available for the placement of visa stamps.

3. Passport-Sized Photographs: Provide recent passport-sized photographs that meet the specified requirements, including size, background color, and facial expression.

4. Travel Itinerary: Include a detailed itinerary of your planned activities in Verona, including accommodation reservations, flight tickets, and any tours or events you intend to attend.

5. Travel Insurance: Proof of travel insurance covering a minimum of €30,000 for medical emergencies, including repatriation, is mandatory.

6. Proof of Accommodation: Provide confirmation of hotel reservations or a letter of invitation from a host in Verona, along with their contact details.

7. Financial Means: Demonstrate proof of sufficient financial means to cover your expenses during your stay in Verona. This may include bank statements, pay stubs, or a letter of sponsorship.

8. Supporting Documents: Depending on the type of visa you're applying for, additional documents such as acceptance letters from educational institutions, employment contracts, or business invitations may be required.

10. Visa Fee Payment: Be prepared to pay the applicable visa fee, which varies depending on your nationality and the type of visa you're applying for.

Remember to check the specific requirements and procedures at the Italian consulate or embassy in your country, as they may have additional requirements or variations in the application process. By ensuring you have all the necessary documents in order, you'll be well-prepared to embark on your Verona adventure.

Types of Visa:

1. Schengen Visa: Verona, as part of Italy, is a member of the Schengen Area. A Schengen visa allows entry into not only Italy but also other Schengen member countries.

2. Tourist Visa (Short-Stay Visa): This visa is suitable for tourists planning to stay in Verona for up to 90 days within a 180-day period. It covers tourism, visiting family or friends, and attending events or conferences.

3. Business Visa (Short-Stay Visa): Designed for business travelers, this visa allows participation in business meetings, conferences, and other related activities. You can stay for up to 3 months in any 6-month period.

4. Student Visa (Long-Stay Visa): If you plan to pursue studies in Verona, a student visa is required. It allows for a stay exceeding 90 days, and you'll need to provide proof of acceptance from a recognized educational institution.

5. Work Visa (Long-Stay Visa): For those seeking employment in Verona, a work visa is necessary. It grants permission to work and reside in the city for an extended period.

Extended Stay

Citizens of most European Union (EU) and Schengen Area countries can stay in Verona for up to 90 days within a 180-day period without a visa. If they wish to stay longer, they must apply for an extension of their stay.

To apply for an extension of stay, they must go to the Questura (police headquarters) in Verona. They will need to bring the following documents:

- A valid passport
- A completed extension of stay application form
- Proof of accommodation for the extended stay
- Proof of sufficient funds to support themselves for the extended stay
- A reason for the extended stay

The Questura will review the application and decide whether to grant the extension. If the extension is granted, the person will be issued with a new residence permit.

You can get an extension of stay application form in Verona at the following locations:

- Questura di Verona: Via Carlo Montanari, 6, 37122 Verona VR, Italy
- Ufficio Anagrafe: Piazza Bra, 1, 37121 Verona VR, Italy
- Ufficio Immigrazione: Via Carlo Montanari, 6, 37122 Verona VR, Italy
- Comune di Verona: Piazza Bra, 1, 37121 Verona VR, Italy

You can also download the extension of stay application form online from the website of the Questura di Verona at https://questure.poliziadistato.it/en/Verona. The website offers two language options: English and Italian.

The processing time for an extension of stay application can vary, so it is important to apply well in advance of your intended departure date.

Prohibited items

The following items are prohibited when entering Italy:

Drugs and narcotics, Firearms and weapons, Explosives and ammunition, Dangerous chemicals and substances, Pornographic and obscene materials, Counterfeit goods, Animals and plants that are not in compliance with Italian regulations.

In addition to the above, the following items are also prohibited when entering Italy:

- Foodstuffs that are not in compliance with Italian regulations
- Alcoholic beverages with an alcohol content of more than 70%
- Tobacco products in excess of the following limits:

400 cigarettes, 200 cigars, 1 kilogram of smoking tobacco and 1 kilogram of chewing tobacco.

If you are bringing any items into Italy that are not on the prohibited list, you should declare them to the customs officials at the port of entry.

Tips For Planning Your Trip to Verona

Here are some insider tips to make your visit to this enchanting city a memorable one:

1. Choose the Right Time of Year: Consider the seasons and choose a time that aligns with your preferences. Spring and early autumn offer pleasant weather with fewer crowds, while summer is bustling with energy.

2. Book Accommodations in Advance: Verona is a popular tourist destination, so it's advisable to book accommodations well in advance to secure your preferred options.

3. Explore Beyond the Main Attractions: While Juliet's House and the Arena are must-sees, don't miss out on exploring the quieter neighbourhoods and hidden gems that Verona has to offer.

4. Learn a Few Basic Italian Phrases: While English is widely spoken, knowing a few basic Italian phrases can go a long way in enhancing your experience and connecting with locals.

5. Consider a Verona Card: The Verona Card gives you free admission to many of Verona's top attractions, including the Roman Arena, Juliet's House, and Castel Vecchio. It also gives you unlimited use of public transportation for 24 or 72 hours.

6. Try Local Cuisine: Venture beyond the tourist areas to discover authentic Veronese cuisine. Don't miss out on specialties like risotto all'Amarone and local wines.

7. Embrace the "Passeggiata": Join the locals in their evening tradition of taking a leisurely stroll along the streets and soaking up the vibrant atmosphere.

8. Take Advantage of Day Trips: Verona's strategic location offers easy access to stunning destinations like Lake Garda, Venice, and the charming town of Soave. Consider day trips to explore the region.

9. Attend a Performance at the Arena: If your visit coincides with the Opera Festival, attending a performance in the Verona Arena is a truly magical experience. Be sure to book tickets in advance.

10. Pack Comfortable Walking Shoes: Verona's cobblestone streets are best explored on foot. Make sure to pack comfortable shoes for hours of leisurely wandering.

12. Leave Room for Spontaneity: While it's great to have an itinerary, leave some room for unexpected discoveries and spontaneous moments that make travel truly special.

13. Plan your sightseeing itinerary: Verona has a lot to offer visitors, so it is important to plan your sightseeing itinerary in advance. Some of the most popular attractions include the Roman Arena, Juliet's House, Castel Vecchio, Piazza delle Erbe, and the Scaligero Bridge.

14. Be prepared for crowds: Verona is a popular tourist destination, so be prepared for crowds, especially at popular attractions like Juliet's House and the Roman Arena. If you are visiting during the peak season, it is a good idea to arrive early in the morning to avoid the crowds.

15. Take your time and enjoy the city: Verona is a beautiful city with a lot to offer visitors. Take your time and enjoy the city's atmosphere, history, and culture.

CHAPTER ONE: GETTING TO VERONA

Verona is accessible through various transportation options. Whether arriving by air, train, or road, reaching this enchanting city is a seamless journey.

Air Travel Options

Verona's international airport, Valerio Catullo Airport (VRN), welcomes travelers from around the world, providing convenient access to this captivating city. Here's a quick guide on how to reach Verona by air from different parts of the globe:

From the UK

There are direct flights from London to Verona Airport (VRN) with British Airways and Ryanair. The estimated duration of the flight is around 2 hours and 15 minutes. For additional options, travelers can consider connecting flights via major European hubs like Frankfurt, Amsterdam, or Zurich.

From the USA

There are no direct flights from the USA to Verona Airport. However, there are many airlines that offer connecting flights to Verona, such as Delta Air Lines, United Airlines, and American Airlines. The total travel time will vary depending on your connecting city.

From Europe

There are direct flights to Verona Airport from many major European cities, such as Paris, Rome, Frankfurt, and Amsterdam. The flight time will vary depending on your departure city

From Canada

There are no direct flights from Canada to Verona Airport. However, there are many airlines that offer connecting flights to Verona, such as Air Canada and WestJet. The total travel time will vary depending on your connecting city.

From Asia

There are no direct flights from most Asian cities to Verona Airport. However, there are many airlines that offer connecting flights to Verona, such as Qatar Airways, Emirates, and Etihad Airways. The total travel time will vary depending on your connecting city and departure city.

Once you arrive at Verona Airport, there are a few ways to get to the city center:

• **Taxi:** Taxis are available outside the airport terminal. The taxi ride to the city center takes approximately 15 minutes and costs around 20 euros.

• **Bus:** There is a bus that runs from the airport to the city center. The bus ride takes approximately 30 minutes and costs around 6 euros.

• **Car rental:** You can rent a car at the airport. This is a good option if you plan on doing a lot of sightseeing outside of Verona

Verona by Train

Verona is a major railway hub in Italy, and there are direct trains to the city from many major Italian and European cities. The train station in Verona is called Verona Porta Nuova, and it is located in the city center.

Here are some tips for getting to Verona by train:

1. Secure your train tickets ahead of time, particularly when you're planning to travel during the busiest season.

2. Arrive at the train station at least 30 minutes before your train is scheduled to depart.

3. Validate your ticket before boarding the train. You can do this by stamping your ticket in one of the validation machines located at the train station.

4. Be aware that some trains may require a reservation. This is especially true for high-speed trains.

5. If you are traveling with luggage, be sure to keep an eye on it at all times.

6. Check the train schedule in advance so that you know when your train is scheduled to depart. You can find the train schedule on the website of the Italian railway company, Trenitalia.

Here are some of the most popular train routes to Verona:

1. From Milan: The train journey from Milan to Verona takes approximately 1 hour and 30 minutes. There are direct trains every hour.

2. From Venice: The train journey from Venice to Verona takes approximately 1 hour and 15 minutes. There are direct trains every hour.

3. From Rome: The train journey from Rome to Verona takes approximately 2 hours and 45 minutes. There are direct trains every hour.

4. From Florence: The train journey from Florence to Verona takes approximately 1 hour and 45 minutes. There are direct trains every hour.

5. From Frankfurt: The train journey from Frankfurt to Verona takes approximately 6 hours and 30 minutes. There are direct trains every day.

6. From Paris: The train journey from Paris to Verona takes approximately 6 hours and 30 minutes. There are direct trains every day.

Once you arrive at Verona Porta Nuova train station, there are a few ways to get to your hotel or other accommodation:

- **Taxi:** Taxis are available outside the train station terminal. The taxi ride to the city center takes approximately 15 minutes and costs around 20 euros.
- **Bus:** There are buses that run from the train station to the city center. The bus ride takes approximately 20 minutes and costs around 2 euros.

- **Walk:** The train station is located in the city center, so it is possible to walk to many hotels and other accommodations.

Getting a train ticket

There are several ways you can get a Verona train ticket. Here are some options:

- **Online:** You can purchase a Verona train ticket online on the Trenitalia website. Trenitalia stands as the primary railway service provider within Italy. You can also purchase a Verona train ticket on the websites of other railway operators, such as Italo and Thello.

- **At the train station:** You can also purchase a Verona train ticket at the train station in Verona. There are ticket machines located throughout the train station. You can also purchase a ticket from a ticket agent.

Choose the right type of ticket for your needs. There are different types of train tickets available, such as full-price tickets, discounted tickets, and season tickets.

By Road, Driving to Verona

Verona is located in the northeastern part of Italy, and it is easily accessible by car from many major European cities. The city is located at the intersection of the A22 Modena-Brennero motorway and the A4 Serenissima motorway.

Here are some tips for getting to Verona by car:

1. Plan your route in advance: This will help you to avoid traffic jams and to find the best route to your destination.

2. Be aware of the speed limits: The speed limit on motorways in Italy is 130 km/h (80 mph).

3. Be prepared for tolls: There are tolls on the A22 and A4 motorways. You can pay the tolls in cash or with a credit card.

4. Purchase a vignette: If you are planning on driving in Italy for more than 10 days, you will need to purchase a vignette. This is a sticker that you must display on your windshield.

5. Be prepared for traffic: Verona is a popular tourist destination, so be prepared for traffic, especially during the peak season (summer).

Here are some of the most popular routes to Verona by car:

1. From Milan: The drive from Milan to Verona takes approximately 1 hour and 30 minutes. Take the A4 motorway towards Venice and exit at Verona Sud.

2. From Venice: The drive from Venice to Verona takes approximately 1 hour and 15 minutes. Take the A4 motorway towards Milan and exit at Verona Nord.

3. From Rome: The drive from Rome to Verona takes approximately 4 hours. Take the A1 motorway towards

Florence and then take the A11 motorway towards Bologna. Take the A13 motorway towards Padua and then take the A4 motorway towards Venice and exit at Verona Sud.

4. From Florence: The drive from Florence to Verona takes approximately 2 hours and 30 minutes. Take the A1 motorway towards Bologna and then take the A13 motorway towards Padua. Take the A4 motorway towards Venice and exit at Verona Sud.

Once you arrive in Verona, there are a few places where you can park your car:

1. Hotels: Many hotels in Verona offer parking for their guests. This is often the most convenient option, but it can also be the most expensive.

2. Public parking garages: There are a number of public parking garages in Verona. These garages are typically located in the city center and are relatively affordable.

3. Street parking: There is also street parking available in Verona, but it can be difficult to find a spot, especially during the peak season.

Here are some additional tips for driving in Verona:

1. Be aware of the ZTL zone: The ZTL zone is a limited traffic zone in the city center of Verona. Only residents and authorized vehicles are allowed in the ZTL zone. If you are driving in Verona, be sure to avoid the ZTL zone, unless you have a special permit.

2. Be prepared for narrow streets: Many of the streets in Verona are narrow and winding. Be careful when driving and be aware of pedestrians.

Travel Itinerary Planner

CHAPTER TWO: EXPLORING VERONA'S NEIGHBOURHOODS

As you embark on a journey through Verona, it's essential to delve into its diverse neighbourhoods. Each district carries its own unique charm, offering a different perspective on this historic city. From the ancient streets of the Old Town to the tranquil banks of the Adige River, this chapter invites you to wander through Verona's neighbourhoods, uncovering hidden treasures and experiencing the city's vibrant tapestry.

Historic Center, The Heart of Verona

Welcome to the pulsating heart of Verona—the Historic Center. This district, a UNESCO World Heritage Site, is where the city's rich history comes to life. Here, ancient Roman ruins blend seamlessly with medieval architecture, creating a captivating atmosphere that beckons explorers. Let's take a closer look at what the Historic Center has to offer:

Amenities you can find at the city center include:

1. Accommodations: The Historic Center boasts a range of charming boutique hotels, bed-and-breakfasts, and guesthouses, offering a cozy retreat within steps of Verona's iconic landmarks.

2. Restaurants and Cafes: From traditional osterias to chic eateries, the Historic Center is a culinary paradise. Indulge in Veronese specialties, accompanied by the region's renowned wines.

3. Shops and Boutiques: Stroll along cobblestone streets, where you'll find an array of artisanal boutiques, fashion shops, and souvenir stores, offering a delightful shopping experience.

4. Cultural Venues: Museums, art galleries, and theaters abound in the Historic Center. Immerse yourself in Verona's vibrant arts scene and explore its rich cultural heritage.

Things to Do in the City Center:

1. Visit Juliet's House (Casa di Giulietta): This iconic site, though fictional in Shakespeare's play, is a must-see. Leave a message on the walls, or ascend to the famed balcony for a moment of reflection.

2. Explore Piazza delle Erbe: This lively square, once a Roman forum, is now a bustling market square. Admire the Baroque architecture and soak in the vibrant atmosphere.

3. Marvel at the Arena di Verona: One of the best-preserved Roman amphitheaters, the Arena hosts spectacular events and concerts. Consider attending a performance for an unforgettable experience.

4. Discover the Arche Scaligere: These Gothic funerary monuments pay tribute to the Scaligeri family, showcasing intricate stonework and historical significance.

Insider Tips:

• **Early Mornings and Late Evenings:** To truly appreciate the charm of the Historic Center, explore it during the early morning or late evening when the crowds thin, and the city takes on a serene ambiance.

• **Wander Aimlessly:** Don't be afraid to get lost in the maze-like streets. Some of the most enchanting discoveries are made off the beaten path.

• **Accessibility:** The Historic Center is pedestrian-friendly, with many attractions within walking distance. It's advisable to wear comfortable footwear for exploring.

• **Opening Hours:** Museums, shops, and restaurants may have varying opening hours, so it's a good idea to check in advance.

• Guided Tours: Consider joining a guided tour for a deeper understanding of the district's history and hidden gems.

San Zeno, Where History Meets Serenity

Nestled on the western bank of the Adige River, the San Zeno neighbourhood is a tranquil oasis that offers a respite from the bustling heart of Verona. Steeped in history and brimming with local charm, this district invites visitors to explore its hidden gems and savor its serene ambiance.

Amenities you can find here include:

1. Basilica di San Zeno Maggiore: The crown jewel of this neighbourhood, this Romanesque masterpiece is a must-visit. Admire its stunning façade, intricate bronze doors, and the serene interiors that house numerous artworks.

2. Piazza San Zeno: This spacious square surrounding the basilica provides a peaceful setting for a leisurely stroll or a moment of reflection. Cafés and quaint shops dot the area, inviting you to soak in the local atmosphere.

3. Local Eateries: San Zeno boasts traditional trattorias and osterias where you can savor authentic Veronese cuisine. Don't miss the opportunity to indulge in local specialties like pastissada de caval (horse meat stew) or risotto with Amarone wine.

Things to Do:

1. Visit the Basilica Cloisters: Step into the serene cloisters of Basilica di San Zeno, where the peaceful atmosphere is perfect for quiet contemplation.

2. Explore San Zeno Bridge: Take a stroll across the nearby San Zeno Bridge for picturesque views of the river and the city skyline.

3. Attend Local Festivals: Check the calendar for any local festivals or events happening in the neighbourhood. These provide an authentic insight into Veronese culture and traditions.

Insider Tips:

- **Early Mornings are Magical:** Visit San Zeno in the early morning to experience the neighbourhood in a serene and quiet state, before the day's activities begin.

- **Engage with Locals:** Strike up a conversation with the friendly residents of San Zeno. They often have fascinating stories and recommendations to share.

- **Sample Local Wines:** Explore the local enotecas (wine shops) for a taste of Verona's renowned wines, including the revered Amarone.

Borgo Trento, The Local's Corner

Nestled just beyond Verona's historic center, Borgo Trento is a neighbourhood that seamlessly blends the city's rich history with a serene ambiance. Here's a comprehensive guide to exploring this charming district:

Amenities you can find here include:

1. Local Markets and Shops: Borgo Trento boasts an array of quaint shops and markets, offering everything from fresh produce to artisanal crafts. Stroll through the streets to discover local treasures.

2. Dining Delights: This neighbourhood is home to an array of authentic trattorias and osterias. Savor Veronese specialties like risotto all'Amarone and indulge in delectable Amarone wines.

3. Green Oasis: The Giardino Giusti, a stunning Renaissance garden, provides a peaceful escape. Admire the meticulously manicured hedges and take in the panoramic views of Verona.

4. Healthcare Facilities: Borgo Trento offers modern medical facilities, including hospitals and pharmacies, ensuring visitors have access to essential healthcare services.

Things to Do:

1. Visit the Giardino Giusti: Wander through this historic garden, which dates back to the 16th century. The intricate labyrinth and scenic terraces offer a tranquil retreat from the city's hustle and bustle.

2. Explore Local Eateries: Dine like a local at Borgo Trento's charming eateries. Don't miss the opportunity to taste the neighbourhood's specialties while enjoying its relaxed, residential atmosphere.

3. Attend a Cooking Class: Immerse yourself in Veronese cuisine by joining a cooking class. Learn the secrets of preparing regional dishes from skilled local chefs.

4. Experience Local Festivals: Keep an eye on the neighbourhood's event calendar. Borgo Trento hosts various festivals and cultural events throughout the year, providing insight into local traditions.

Insider Tips:

- **Early Morning Strolls:** Take advantage of the peaceful mornings to explore Borgo Trento's streets. The soft morning light casts a magical glow on the neighbourhood's historic architecture.

- **Explore the Side Streets:** Don't hesitate to venture off the main roads. Borgo Trento's hidden alleys often reveal charming surprises, from quaint shops to picturesque courtyards.

- **Engage with Locals:** Strike up conversations with the friendly residents. They may share invaluable tips and insights about the neighbourhood's hidden gems.

- **Accessibility:** Borgo Trento is easily accessible from the city center, either by a leisurely stroll or a short taxi ride. It's approximately a 20-minute walk from Piazza Bra.

- **Public Transportation:** The neighbourhood is well-served by buses, making it easy to navigate to and from other parts of Verona.

- **Safety:** Borgo Trento is considered a safe neighbourhood, with a welcoming atmosphere. As with any travel, it's advisable to exercise normal precautions.

Travel Itinerary Planner

_____

_____

_____

_____

_____

_____

_____

_____

_____

_____

_____

_____

_____

CHAPTER THREE: THINGS TO DO IN VERONA

Verona, with its timeless charm and rich history, offers a treasure trove of experiences for visitors. This chapter is your gateway to discovering the myriad activities that make Verona a destination like no other. From immersing yourself in Shakespearean romance to savoring the flavors of Veronese cuisine, join me as we unravel the endless possibilities that await in this captivating city.

Must-See Attractions in Verona

Verina is adorned with architectural marvels, picturesque piazzas, and cultural treasures. Let's explore the must-see wonders that make Verona a destination unlike any other.

Juliet's House, Love and Legends

Juliet's House, or "Casa di Giulietta" in Italian, is an iconic landmark in Verona, forever entwined with Shakespeare's timeless tragedy. The house is said to have been the home of Juliet Capulet, one of the characters in

Shakespeare's Romeo and Juliet. This 13th-century residence, with its charming Gothic architecture and iconic balcony, draws visitors from around the world, eager to experience the romantic ambiance that permeates its walls. Located Via Cappello, 23, 37121 Verona VR, Italy.

Activities:

1. Balcony Gazing: Stand on the legendary balcony where Juliet is said to have spoken sweet words with Romeo. It's a must for romantics and Shakespeare enthusiasts.

2. Love Notes: The courtyard is adorned with love notes left by visitors. Leave your own message or seek inspiration from the heartfelt expressions of love.

3. Museum Exploration: Discover the history and artifacts within the museum, which provides insights into the era of the Montague and Capulet families.

Other necessary information for tourist:

- Entrance fee: The entrance fee to Juliet's House is 6 euros for adults and 4 euros for children.
Photo fee: The fee to take a photo with Juliet's statue is 2 euros.

- Contact details: Phone number, +39 045 806 4465
Email address, info@cas Giulietta.it

- Opening hours: April to September, 8:30 AM to 7:30 PM and October to March, 8:30 AM to 6:00 PM

- Guided tours are available for a deeper exploration of the house and its history.

- The house tends to be more crowded during peak tourist hours, so visiting early in the morning or later in the evening can provide a more intimate experience.

- The house is not accessible to wheelchairs and visitors are not allowed to touch the Juliet statue.

Verona Arena, Epicenter of Entertainment

The Verona Arena, an ancient Roman amphitheater, stands as an architectural marvel and a testament to Verona's rich history. Constructed in the 1st century AD, it once hosted gladiatorial contests and grand spectacles, now serving as an iconic venue for cultural events. Don't miss the opportunity to witness the magic of this iconic venue during your Verona adventure. Located at Piazza Brà, 1, 37121 Verona VR, Italy.

Activities:

Today, the Arena hosts a myriad of events, including the renowned Opera Festival, concerts, and theatrical performances. Visitors can also explore its ancient corridors and ascend to the terraces for panoramic views of Verona.

Other necessary information for tourists

- Admission varies depending on the event or exhibition. For regular visits, tickets are approximately €10-12. Special events may have different pricing.

- Contact Details:
Phone: +39 045 800 5151
Email: info@arenadiverona.it
Website: City of Verona tourism website: https://www.visitverona.it/en

- The Arena's hours fluctuate based on events and seasons. Generally, it's open from 9:00 AM to 6:30 PM for visits, but it's closed on Mondays.

- Guided tours are available, offering in-depth insights into the Arena's history and architecture.
- It's advisable to check the official website or contact the Arena for event schedules and ticket availability.
- Visitors with reduced mobility are accommodated with special access points and services.

- The Verona Arena is a UNESCO World Heritage Site.
- The Arena is best reached by public transportation.
- There are several restaurants and cafes located near the Arena.

Piazza delle Erbe, Market Square Magic

Piazza delle Erbe, once the heart of Roman Verona, now stands as a lively marketplace surrounded by stunning medieval and Renaissance buildings. Vibrant stalls, colorful awnings, and a central fountain create an atmosphere that brims with energy and history. Located in the heart of Verona's historic center, Piazza delle Erbe is easily accessible from various points in the city. It's a central hub for both locals and tourists alike.

Activities:

1. Market Exploration: Stroll through the bustling market stalls offering a delightful array of local goods, from fresh produce to handcrafted souvenirs.

2. People-Watching: Find a café along the perimeter and soak in the lively atmosphere. Watch locals and visitors alike as they go about their day.

3. Historical Appreciation: Admire the surrounding architecture, including the striking Torre dei Lamberti and the exquisite frescoes of Palazzo Maffei.

4. Visiting the monuments: Piazza delle Erbe is surrounded by several historic monuments, including the Palazzo della Ragione and the Casa Mazzanti.

5. Enjoying a meal or drink: Piazza delle Erbe is surrounded by cafes and restaurants where visitors can enjoy a meal or drink while taking in the atmosphere of the square.

Other necessary information for tourists

- Piazza delle Erbe is open to the public 24 hours a day, 7 days a week.

- Piazza delle Erbe can be very crowded, especially during the summer months. Visitors should be prepared for crowds and take precautions against petty theft.

- The square is cobbled, so visitors should wear comfortable shoes.

- There are several public restrooms located near Piazza delle Erbe.

- The square is easily navigable for individuals with mobility challenges, but the cobblestone surface may pose some difficulties.

- Visit in the morning for a quieter experience before the market gets into full swing. Don't forget to haggle a bit with the vendors for a true Italian market experience.

- Consider joining a guided tour to gain deeper insights into the history and significance of Piazza delle Erbe.

Piazza delle Erbe is not only a marketplace but a living testament to Verona's vibrant past and present. Whether you're browsing the stalls, sipping coffee, or simply taking in the scenery, this square promises an enriching experience for all who visit.

Castelvecchio, A Fortress of History

Castelvecchio, a majestic medieval fortress, stands as a testament to Verona's rich history. Built in the 14th century, this architectural gem boasts impressive battlements and a captivating stone bridge spanning the Adige River. Today, Castelvecchio is a museum that houses a collection of art and artifacts. The collection includes paintings, sculptures, weapons, and armor. The museum also has a library and a collection of musical instruments.

Here are some of the activities that can be done at Castelvecchio:

1. Art and History Exploration: Wander through the castle's museum, housing an extensive collection of medieval and Renaissance art, including works by local masters.

2. Admire Architectural Grandeur: Marvel at the castle's imposing structure, fortified walls, and the picturesque Ponte Scaligero bridge.

3. Enjoy Scenic Views: Climb the castle's towers for panoramic views of Verona and the Adige River.

4. Take a guided tour: Guided tours are available in English and Italian.

5. Attend a concert: The castle often hosts concerts and other events.

6. Visit the library: The library has a collection of books on a variety of topics, including art, history, and literature.

7. Visit the collection of musical instruments: The collection of musical instruments includes instruments from all over the world.

Other necessary information for tourists

- The entrance fee for Castelvecchio is 8 euros. Discounts are accessible to students, seniors, and group patrons.
- Contact details: The address of Castelvecchio is Via Romeo, 1, 37121 Verona VR, Italy. The phone number is +39 045 803 3311.
- Castelvecchio is open from Tuesday to Sunday from 8:30am to 7:30pm. It is closed on Mondays
- The castle is wheelchair accessible, ensuring inclusivity for all visitors.
- Photography without flash is allowed to capture the castle's timeless beauty.
- There is a cafe on-site where you can purchase food and drinks.
- There is a gift shop on-site where you can purchase souvenirs.

Ponte Pietra, Bridge to the Past

Ponte Pietra, translating to "Stone Bridge," is a Roman marvel that spans the gentle waters of the Adige River. Its ancient stones whisper tales of centuries gone by, making it one of Verona's most cherished landmarks. Located in the heart of Verona, Ponte Pietra gracefully connects the bustling historic center with the tranquil neighbourhood of Borgo Trento.

Strolling across Ponte Pietra offers a picturesque view of Verona's skyline, making it an ideal spot for photography and contemplative moments. Additionally, the bridge provides access to the peaceful paths along the riverbanks.

Ponte Pietra is accessible year-round, allowing visitors to appreciate its beauty at any time. The bridge remains open 24 hours a day, offering a serene escape in both daylight and under the city's illuminated night sky.

Other necessary information for tourists

- The bridge is made of limestone and is approximately 200 meters long.
- The bridge has five arches and is decorated with Roman statues.
- The bridge is a popular spot for weddings and other special events.
- The bridge is a popular spot for birdwatching.
- The bridge is accessible by foot, and while there are some stairs on either end, there are also ramps available for those with mobility challenges.
- Various guided tours of Verona often include Ponte Pietra as a highlight, providing historical context and interesting anecdotes.
- Ponte Pietra offers a spectacular vantage point for watching the sunset over Verona, creating a truly magical experience.

Basilica di San Zeno Maggiore

The Basilica di San Zeno Maggiore is a Romanesque church in Verona, Italy. It is one of the most important

Romanesque churches in Italy and is dedicated to Saint Zeno of Verona. The church was built in the 11th and 12th centuries and is known for its beautiful architecture and its important collection of art and artifacts. The Basilica di San Zeno Maggiore is located in the historic center of Verona, Italy. It is a short walk from the Verona Arena and other popular tourist attractions.

Visitors to the Basilica di San Zeno Maggiore can enjoy the following activities:

1. Admire the architecture: The Basilica di San Zeno Maggiore is one of the most important Romanesque churches in Italy. Visitors can admire the beautiful architecture of the church, including its rose window, its two towers, and its interior.

2. See the art and artifacts: The Basilica di San Zeno Maggiore houses a collection of important art and artifacts, including a bronze crucifix by Benedetto Antelami and a painting of the Virgin and Child by Alessandro Turchi.

3. Attend a service: The Basilica di San Zeno Maggiore is still an active church, and visitors can attend a service to experience the atmosphere of the church.

Other necessary Information for tourists

- Admission to the Basilica di San Zeno Maggiore is free. However, there is a suggested donation of 2 euros.
- The Basilica di San Zeno Maggiore is located at Piazza San Zeno, 2, 37123 Verona, Italy. The phone number is +39 045 800 7643.
- The Basilica di San Zeno Maggiore is open from 9:00 AM to 12:30 PM and from 2:00 PM to 6:00 PM.
- Dress modestly, as it's a place of worship.
- Photography may be restricted in certain areas, so it's best to check with the staff.
- Guided tours are available for a more in-depth exploration of the basilica's history and art.
- The church is wheelchair accessible.
- There is a gift shop in the church where you can purchase souvenirs.

Giardino Giusti, A Green Oasis in the City

Giardino Giusti is a beautiful Italian Renaissance garden located in the heart of Verona, Italy. The garden was designed in the 16th century by Andrea Giusti and is considered to be one of the finest examples of its kind in Italy. Located Via Giardino Giusti 2, 37121 Verona VR, Italy

Activities:

1. Visit the garden: The garden is open to the public and is a great place to relax and enjoy the natural beauty of Verona.

2. Take a tour: There are guided tours of the garden available, which are a great way to learn about the history and design of the garden.

3. Attend a concert or event: The garden is also used for concerts and other events throughout the year.

4. Have a picnic: The garden is a great place to have a picnic lunch or dinner.

Other necessary information for tourists

● Cost: Garden admission, €10 and guided tour, €12

●   Contact   details:
Website:https://giardinogiusti.com/article/11305/il-giardi no/?lan=en

Email: info@giardino giusti.it

Phone: +39 045 800 5446

● Opening hours: April-October 9am-7pm and November-March 9am-5pm

● The garden is accessible to people with disabilities.

● There is a cafe and restaurant located on the grounds of the garden.

● It's recommended to wear comfortable footwear for exploring the garden's terraces and pathways.

Museo di Castelvecchio, Art and Artifacts

Museo di Castelvecchio is a museum in Verona, Italy, located in the eponymous medieval castle. The museum houses a collection of art and artifacts from the Middle Ages to the 19th century, including paintings, sculptures, arms and armor, and other objects.

Museo di Castelvecchio is one of the most important museums in Verona, and it is a must-see for anyone interested in art and history. The museum is located in a beautiful medieval castle, and the collection is well-curated and displayed.

Visitors to Museo di Castelvecchio can expect to see a wide variety of art and artifacts, including:

1. Paintings from the Middle Ages to the 19th century, including works by Paolo Veronese, Andrea Mantegna, and Titian

2. Sculptures from the Middle Ages to the Renaissance

3. Arms and armor from the Middle Ages to the 19th century

4. Other objects, such as tapestries, furniture, and ceramics

Other necessary information for tourists

- The museum also offers a variety of educational programs and events, including guided tours, workshops, and lectures.
- The cost of admission to Museo di Castelvecchio is €10 for adults, €8 for seniors and students, and free for children under 18.
- Museo di Castelvecchio is open Tuesday through Sunday from 8:30am to 7:30pm. The museum is closed on Mondays.
- Museo di Castelvecchio is wheelchair accessible.
- The museum has a cafe and a gift shop.
- There is a parking garage located near the museum.
- The museum offers a free audio guide in English, Italian, French, German, Spanish, and Russian.

- There are a number of restaurants and cafes located near the museum.

Santa Anastasia, A Gothic Marvel

Santa Anastasia, situated in Verona, Italy, stands as an exemplary specimen of Gothic architecture. As the largest church in the city and a designated UNESCO World Heritage Site, it holds immense cultural and historical significance. The foundation of this remarkable church was laid by the Dominican Order in the 13th century, commencing a construction process that spanned over two centuries, culminating in its consecration in 1481.

Exemplifying the quintessence of Gothic design, the church showcases distinctive features including pointed arches, ribbed vaults, and resplendent stained glass windows. The facade, adorned with statues paying homage to saints and martyrs, is a testament to the artistry of its creators.

Within, the church offers a spacious and light-filled interior. The nave is elegantly partitioned into four aisles by a succession of pointed arches, evoking a sense of grandeur. Towards the eastern terminus, the choir is adorned with magnificent frescoes courtesy of the esteemed artist Andrea Mantegna. Santa Anastasia stands not only as a place of worship but also as a living testament to the enduring beauty of Gothic architecture.

The church houses a number of works of art and artifacts, including:

- Frescoes by Andrea Mantegna in the choir
- Tomb of Cansignorio della Scala, a 14th-century ruler of Verona
- Tomb of Giovanni della Scala, a 14th-century ruler of Verona
- Altarpiece by Giovanni Bellini
- Sculptures by Andrea della Robbia

Santa Anastasia is open to the public for visits. The church is located in the historic center of Verona and is easy to access by foot or by public transportation.

The church offers a free audio guide in English, Italian, French, German, Spanish, and Russian.

Torre dei Lamberti

The Torre dei Lamberti, situated in Verona, Italy, stands as a medieval marvel. This iconic edifice is not only one of the city's most recognized landmarks but also a favored destination for tourists. Erected in the 12th century under the patronage of the Lamberti family, renowned merchants of Verona, the tower initially served as a defensive stronghold. However, its purpose transformed over time, evolving into a resounding belfry.

Constructed from a combination of durable brick and sturdy stone, the tower proudly soars to a height of 84 meters. Its foundation takes on a square form, harmoniously divided into five distinct levels. At its pinnacle lies a belfry, which houses three resonant bells, adding a melodic charm to the city's skyline.

Other necessary information for tourists

- Torre dei Lamberti is open to the public for visits. Visitors can climb the 368 steps to the top of the tower for stunning views of Verona.
- There is a lift that can take visitors to the top of the tower, but it is not wheelchair accessible.
- The tower is open from 8:30 am to 7:30 pm, except on Mondays.
- The cost of admission is €6 for adults, €4 for seniors and students, and free for children under 6.
- The tower is located in the Piazza dei Signori, the main square in Verona.
- The tower is said to be haunted by the ghost of a woman who was imprisoned in the tower in the 14th century.
- The tower was used as a filming location for the 1996 film "Romeo + Juliet".

Ponte Scaligero

The Ponte Scaligero, also known as the Scaligero Bridge, is a medieval architectural gem situated in Verona, Italy. This renowned landmark stands as a testament to the city's rich history and draws inquisitive tourists from far and wide. Constructed during the 14th century under the patronage of the ruling Scaligeri family, the bridge originally served as a defensive structure. Today, it has transformed into a beloved pedestrian walkway, offering breathtaking views of the city.

Crafted from a combination of durable brick and stone, the Ponte Scaligero spans an impressive 37 meters. The bridge's graceful arches are flanked by sturdy towers on either side, their summits adorned with ornate merlons, providing both structural support and an aesthetic flourish. This architectural marvel is a testament to the ingenuity of its creators and stands as an enduring symbol of Verona's medieval legacy.

Other necessary information for tourists

- Ponte Scaligero is open to the public for visits. Visitors can walk across the bridge and enjoy the views of the Adige River and the city of Verona.
- The bridge is located in the heart of Verona and is easily accessible by foot or by public transportation.
- The bridge is wheelchair accessible.
- The bridge is open from 8:30 am to 7:30 pm, except on Mondays.
- The cost of admission is €6 for adults, €4 for seniors and students, and free for children under 6.
- The bridge is located near the Castelvecchio, a medieval castle that is now a museum.
- The bridge is said to be haunted by the ghost of a woman who was executed on the bridge in the 14th century.
- The bridge was used as a filming location for the 1996 film "Romeo + Juliet".

Piazza dei Signori

Piazza dei Signori, also known as "Lord's Square," is a historic civic square nestled in the heart of Verona, Italy. This elegant square has played witness to centuries of political and cultural events, making it a significant hub of the city.

Surrounded by splendid Renaissance palaces, including the Palazzo della Ragione and the Loggia del Consiglio, Piazza dei Signori exudes an air of timeless grandeur. The square's architecture showcases a harmonious blend of Gothic and Renaissance styles, offering a visual feast for visitors. Located via Piazza dei Signori, 37121 Verona VR, Italy.

Visitors can take leisurely strolls, soak in the architectural splendor, and perhaps pause to enjoy a coffee at one of the charming cafes that line the square.

Notable Sights include:

- Palazzo della Ragione: A majestic palace with a prominent clock tower, known for its historic significance in Verona.
- Loggia del Consiglio: A striking open-air structure adorned with classical statues, offering a glimpse into Verona's political history.

Duomo di Verona

The Duomo di Verona, also known as Verona Cathedral, stands as an architectural jewel in the heart of the city. This sacred edifice is a striking embodiment of Verona's rich religious heritage and a testament to the skill and devotion of its creators.

The cathedral's façade is an intricate blend of Romanesque and Gothic styles, adorned with delicate sculptures and reliefs that tell stories of faith and devotion. The grandeur of its marble exterior is matched only by the serene beauty found within. Located via Piazza Duomo, 21, 37121 Verona VR, Italy.

Visitors can explore the cathedral's interior, which houses a collection of significant religious art and artifacts. Ascend the bell tower for panoramic views of the city, or simply find solace within the hallowed halls.

Notable Sights include Arche Scaligere, Adjacent to the cathedral, these Gothic-style tombs pay tribute to the powerful Scaligeri family that once ruled Verona.

The cathedral often hosts religious ceremonies, offering visitors an opportunity to witness local traditions and experience the spiritual ambiance of the space. Visitors are requested to dress respectfully, taking into account the religious significance of the site.

The Duomo di Verona is not only a place of worship but a living testament to the enduring faith and cultural legacy of Verona. Its stunning architecture and spiritual ambiance invite visitors to reflect on the deep history and profound significance that this sacred space holds.

Activities for Families

Verona is a city that welcomes families with open arms, offering a plethora of activities tailored to entertain both young and old. From exploring ancient amphitheaters to strolling through charming parks, there's something for everyone. This section is your guide to family-friendly adventures in Verona, ensuring cherished memories for all.

Gardaland

Gardaland is a theme park in Castelnuovo del Garda, Verona, Italy. It is the most popular theme park in Italy and one of the most popular in Europe. The park is divided into different themed areas, including Adventure, Fantasy, Magic, and Adrenaline. There are rides and attractions for all ages, from gentle rides for young children to thrilling rides for adults.

Here are some of the things you can do at Gardaland:

1. Ride the roller coasters: Gardaland has some of the best roller coasters in Europe, including Blue Tornado, Oblivion, and Raptor.

2. Visit the aquarium: Gardaland SEA LIFE Aquarium is home to over 5,000 marine creatures, including sharks, penguins, and sea turtles.

3. See a show: Gardaland offers a variety of shows, including magic shows, acrobatic shows, and animal shows.

4. Meet your favorite characters: Gardaland is home to a number of characters from popular cartoons and movies, including Peppa Pig, Garfield, and Scooby-Doo.

5. Play games: Gardaland has a number of arcade games and other games that you can play for prizes.

Gardaland is open from April to October. The park is busiest during the summer months, so it is best to visit during the shoulder season (April-May and September-October) if possible.

The cost of admission to Gardaland varies depending on the time of year. A one-day ticket for adults costs €40 in the spring and fall and €45 in the summer. Children under 10 years old receive a discount. You can also purchase a two-day ticket for €55 or a three-day ticket for €65.

Other necessary information for tourists

- Gardaland is located about 30 minutes from Verona by car. There is also a bus that runs from Verona to Gardaland.
- Gardaland is a wheelchair-accessible park.
- Tel: +39 045 644977
- There are a number of restaurants and cafes located inside the park.
- Gardaland has a number of shops where you can buy souvenirs and other items.
- Take advantage of the Fast Track system to skip the lines for popular rides.
- Take breaks throughout the day, especially if you are traveling with young children.

Sea Life Aquarium

There is a Gardaland SEA LIFE Aquarium located inside Gardaland in Castelnuovo del Garda, which is about a 20-minute drive from Verona.

The Gardaland SEA LIFE Aquarium is home to over 5,000 creatures from over 100 different species. Visitors can see sharks, rays, penguins, sea turtles, and more. The aquarium offers several engaging displays, including a touch tank and an immersive shark tunnel experience.

Here are some of the activities you can do at the Gardaland SEA LIFE Aquarium:

1. See sharks, rays, penguins, sea turtles, and more
2. Visit the interactive exhibits, such as the touch tank and the shark tunnel
3 Learn about the different species of marine life and their habitats
4. Watch educational talks and demonstrations
5. Attend special events, such as feeding time and behind-the-scenes tours

The cost of admission to the Gardaland SEA LIFE Aquarium is €18 for adults, €15 for children aged 3-15, and free for children under 3.

Other necessary information for tourists

- The aquarium is open from 10:00am to 6:00pm, every day of the year.
- The aquarium is wheelchair accessible.
- Contact +39 045 6449788
- There is a cafe and a gift shop located inside the aquarium.
- There is a large car park located next to the aquarium.
- The aquarium offers a free audio guide in English, Italian, French, German, Spanish, and Russian.

Acquapark Verona

Acquapark Verona is a water park located in Pescantina, Verona, Italy. It is the largest water park in the Veneto region and one of the largest in Italy. The park has a variety of slides, pools, and other attractions for all ages.

Here are some of the most popular attractions at Acquapark Verona:

1. Kamikaze: This high-speed slide sends riders down a steep drop at speeds of up to 70 km/h.

2. Space Bowl: This funnel-shaped slide spins riders around and around before sending them out into a pool at the bottom.

3. Black Hole: This dark and twisty slide takes riders on a wild ride through a series of tunnels and drops.

4. Wave Pool: This large pool features artificial waves that are perfect for surfing and bodyboarding.

5. Lazy River: This winding river is perfect for relaxing and floating along.

Acquapark Verona also has a number of pools for children, including a toddler pool, a baby pool, and a water playground.

The park is open from May to September and is busiest during the summer months. It is best to visit during the shoulder season (May-June and September-October) if possible to avoid the crowds.

The cost of admission to Acquapark Verona varies depending on the time of year and the age of the visitor. A one-day ticket for adults costs €25 in the spring and fall and €30 in the summer. Children under 10 years old receive a discount. Contact +39 045 715 1401

Other necessary information for tourists

- Acquapark Verona is located about 10 minutes from Verona by car. There is also a bus that runs from Verona to Acquapark Verona.
- Acquapark Verona is a wheelchair-accessible park.
- There are a number of restaurants and cafes located inside the park.
- Acquapark Verona has a number of shops where you can buy souvenirs and other items.

- Acquapark Verona offers a range of eateries and snack bars, ensuring you stay energized throughout your aquatic adventures.
- The park prioritizes guest safety, with trained lifeguards on duty and strict adherence to safety guidelines.

Movieland Park

Movieland Park, situated in Lazise, Verona, Italy, is a captivating theme park that celebrates the enchanting realm of cinema and television. Within the park's borders, visitors can indulge in a diverse range of entertainment options, encompassing thrilling roller coasters, refreshing water rides, and captivating shows.

Here are some of the most popular attractions at Movieland Park:

1. Hollywood Action Stunt Show: This show features stuntmen and women performing daring stunts from famous movies and TV shows.

2. Speed Machines: This roller coaster takes riders on a high-speed journey through a series of loops and turns.

3. The Flying Island: This water ride takes riders on a thrilling journey through a series of waterfalls and splash zones.

4. Kung Fu Academy: This interactive show teaches visitors the basics of kung fu.

5. 4D Experience: This 4D cinema takes viewers on a thrilling adventure through a variety of famous movies and TV shows.

Movieland Park is open from May to September and is busiest during the summer months. It is best to visit during the shoulder season (May-June and September-October) if possible to avoid the crowds.

The cost of admission to Movieland Park varies depending on the time of year and the age of the visitor. A one-day ticket for adults costs €32 in the spring and fall and €35 in the summer. Children under 10 years old receive a discount.

Other necessary information for tourists

• Contact details: Movieland Park, Via Fossalta, 56 37017 Lazise (VR), Italy. Phone, +39 045 755 0505.

• Movieland Park is located about 20 minutes from Verona by car. There is also a bus that runs from Verona to Movieland Park.

• Movieland Park is a wheelchair-accessible park.

• There are a number of restaurants and cafes located inside the park.

• Movieland Park has a number of shops where you can buy souvenirs and other items.

Canevaworld Aquapark

Canevaworld Aquapark is a water park located in Lazise, Verona, Italy. It is one of the most popular water parks in Italy and is known for its Caribbean-themed atmosphere. The park has a variety of slides, pools, and other attractions for all ages.

Here are some of the things you can do at Canevaworld Aquapark:

1. Ride the slides: Canevaworld Aquapark has a variety of slides for all ages and thrill levels. Some of the most popular slides include the Kamikaze, the Black Hole, and the Space Bowl.

2. Relax in the pools: Canevaworld Aquapark has a variety of pools for all ages, including a wave pool, a lazy river, and a children's pool.

3. Enjoy the entertainment: Canevaworld Aquapark offers a variety of entertainment throughout the day, including live music, shows, and games.

Other necessary information for tourists

- Canevaworld Aquapark is open from May to September from 10:00 AM to 6:00 PM.
- The cost of admission to Canevaworld Aquapark varies depending on the time of year and the age of the visitor. A one-day ticket for adults costs €25 in the

spring and fall and €30 in the summer. Children under 10 years old receive a discount.

- Contact details: Canevaworld Aqua Park Via Fossalta, 58 37017 Lazise (VR), Italy Tel: +39 045 644 9777.

- Canevaworld Aquapark is located about 20 minutes from Verona by car. There is also a bus that runs from Verona to Canevaworld Aquapark.

- Canevaworld Aquapark is a wheelchair-accessible park.

- There are a number of restaurants and cafes located inside the park.

- Canevaworld Aquapark has a number of shops where you can buy souvenirs and other items.

Sigurtà Garden Park

Sigurtà Garden Park is a public park in Valeggio sul Mincio, Verona, Italy. It is one of the most popular tourist destinations in the region and is known for its beautiful gardens and flowers. Sigurtà Garden Park is located about 20 km from Verona and is easy to access by car or bus.

Sigurtà Garden Park has a variety of things to offer visitors, including:

1. Explore the gardens: The park is home to a variety of gardens, including a rose garden, a water garden, and a tulip garden.

2. Take a boat ride: The park offers boat rides on its lakes and canals.

3. Visit the castle: The park is home to a 14th-century castle that can be visited by tourists.

4. Have a picnic: The park has a number of picnic areas where visitors can enjoy their own food and drinks.

Other necessary information for tourists

- Sigurtà Garden Park is open from March to November, from 9:00 AM to 7:00 PM.
- The cost of admission to Sigurtà Garden Park varies depending on the time of year and the age of the visitor. A one-day ticket for adults costs €16 in the spring and

fall and €18 in the summer. Kids aged 13 and under are eligible for a reduced rate.

• Contact details: Sigurtà Garden Park Via Cavour, 1 37067 Valeggio sul Mincio (VR), Italy Tel: +39 045 6371033.

• The park has a number of restaurants and cafes.

• The park has a gift shop where you can buy souvenirs.

Parco Natura Viva

Parco Natura Viva is a zoological park located in Bussolengo, Verona, Italy. It is divided into two areas: the Safari Park and the Fauna Park. The Safari Park can be explored by car, while the Fauna Park can be explored on foot. Parco Natura Viva is located about 20 minutes from Verona by car. There is also a bus that runs from Verona to Parco Natura Viva.

Here are some of the things you can do at Parco Natura Viva:

1. See the animals in the Safari Park: The Safari Park is home to a variety of animals, including lions, tigers, elephants, and giraffes. You can drive through the Safari Park in your own car or take a guided tour.

2. Walk through the Fauna Park: The Fauna Park is home to a variety of animals from all over the world, including gorillas, chimpanzees, penguins, and polar bears. You can walk through the Fauna Park at your own pace or take a guided tour.

3. Feed the animals: At Parco Natura Viva, you can feed some of the animals, such as giraffes and goats.

4. Learn about the animals: Parco Natura Viva offers a variety of educational programs and activities, such as animal talks and behind-the-scenes tours.

Other necessary information for tourists

• Parco Natura Viva is open from March to December. The operating hours are subject to change throughout the year. For the latest and most accurate details, I recommend visiting the website or calling.

- The cost of admission to Parco Natura Viva varies depending on the time of year and the age of the visitor. A one-day ticket for adults costs €25 in the spring and fall and €30 in the summer. Children under 10 years old receive a discount.

- Contact details: Parco Natura Viva Località Quercia 37014 Bussolengo (VR), Italy Tel: +39 045 717 0113.

- Parco Natura Viva is a wheelchair-accessible park.
- There are a number of restaurants and cafes located inside the park.
- Parco Natura Viva has a number of shops where you can buy souvenirs and other items.

Jungle Adventure Park

Jungle Adventure Park is an outdoor adventure park located in San Zeno di Montagna, about 20 minutes from Verona, Italy. The park is set in a beautiful forest and features a variety of rope courses, zip lines, and other challenges for all ages and abilities.

Jungle Adventure Park offers a variety of activities for visitors of all ages and abilities, including:

1. Rope courses: There are a variety of rope courses to choose from, ranging in difficulty from easy to challenging. The courses feature a variety of obstacles, such as bridges, nets, and zip lines.

2. Zip lines: Jungle Adventure Park has a variety of zip lines, including some of the longest and fastest zip lines in Italy.

3. Other challenges: The park also has a number of other challenges, such as climbing walls, balance beams, and Tarzan swings.

Other necessary information for tourists

- Jungle Adventure Park is open from April to October, from 9:00am to 6:00pm. The park is closed on Mondays.

- The cost of admission to Jungle Adventure Park varies depending on the age of the visitor and the activities they wish to participate in. A one-day ticket for adults costs €25, and a one-day ticket for children costs €20. Discounts are also offered to groups and families.

- Contact details: Jungle Adventure Park Strada per Lumini, Pineta Sperane 37010 San Zeno di Montagna (VR), Italy Tel: +39 045 6289306.

- The park places a strong emphasis on safety, with trained instructors, top-quality equipment, and thorough safety briefings before embarking on the courses.

- Participants must meet certain height and age requirements to participate in specific activities. It is advisable to review these guidelines before visiting.

Verona Botanical Garden

The Verona Botanical Garden is a beautiful oasis in the heart of the city. It is located in the Veronetta district, just a short walk from the city center. The garden is home to a wide variety of plants from all over the world, including many rare and endangered species.

There are many things to see and do at the Verona Botanical Garden. Visitors can wander through the various gardens, explore the greenhouses, and learn about the different plants on display. The garden provides an array of educational programs and events that take place across all seasons annually.

Here are some of the things you can do at the Verona Botanical Garden:

1. Visit the rose garden: The rose garden is one of the most popular attractions in the garden. It is home to over 1,000 rose bushes of different varieties.

3. Explore the greenhouse: The greenhouse is home to a variety of tropical plants, including orchids, cacti, and succulents.

4. Visit the medicinal plant garden: The medicinal plant garden contains a variety of plants that have been used for medicinal purposes throughout history.

5. Take a walk through the bamboo forest: The bamboo forest is a unique and peaceful place to relax and enjoy the beauty of nature.

6. Visit the Japanese garden: The Japanese garden is a beautiful and serene space that is perfect for meditation and contemplation.

Other necessary information for tourists

- The Verona Botanical Garden is open from 9:00am to 7:00pm, seven days a week.

- The cost of admission to the Verona Botanical Garden is €6 for adults and €4 for children under 12 years old.

- Contact details: Orto Botanico di Verona Via Carlo Preti, 5 37121 Verona, Italy Tel: +39 045 803 4029

- There are a number of benches and tables located throughout the garden where visitors can relax and have a picnic.

- The garden has a small gift shop where visitors can purchase souvenirs and plants.

- The garden is a popular spot for birdwatching. There are a variety of bird species that can be seen in the garden, including woodpeckers, finches, and tits.

- Guided tours are available for those seeking a deeper understanding of the garden's history and botanical significance.

Museo Archeologico del Teatro Romano

The Museo Archeologico del Teatro Romano (Archaeological Museum of the Roman Theatre) is a museum in Verona, Italy, located in the former convent of the Gesuati, next to the Roman Theatre. It is one of the most important archaeological museums in Italy, housing a collection of artifacts from the city's Roman and medieval periods.

The Museo Archeologico del Teatro Romano is located in the heart of Verona, on the banks of the Adige River. The museum is easy to access by foot, bike, or car.

Visitors to the Museo Archeologico del Teatro Romano can expect to see a wide variety of artifacts, including:

1. Sculptures from the Roman period, including statues of gods, emperors, and other notable figures

2. Inscriptions from the Roman period, including tombstones, dedications, and other public and private documents

3. Mosaics from the Roman period, including geometric and figurative mosaics from homes, baths, and other buildings.

4. Pottery from the Roman period, including vessels used for everyday life, cooking, and religious rituals.

5. Metalwork from the Roman period, including tools, weapons, and jewelry

6. Coins from the Roman period, including gold, silver, and bronze coins

7. Artifacts from the medieval period, including weapons, armor, jewelry, and pottery
The museum also offers a variety of educational programs and events, including guided tours, workshops, and lectures.

Other necessary information for tourists

• The Museo Archeologico del Teatro Romano is open from Tuesday to Sunday from 8:30am to 7:30pm. The museum is closed on Mondays.

• The cost of admission to the Museo Archeologico del Teatro Romano is €10 for adults, €8 for seniors and students, and free for children under 6.

- Contact details: Museo Archeologico del Teatro Romano Piazza del Castelvecchio, 2 37121 Verona, Italy Tel: +39 045 711 0129.

- The Museo Archeologico del Teatro Romano is wheelchair accessible.
- There is a parking garage located near the museum.

- If you are visiting during the peak season (summer), it is a good idea to purchase your tickets in advance to avoid long lines.

- Guided tours, available in various languages, provide in-depth exploration of the museum's treasures.

- Temporary exhibitions and special events are hosted throughout the year, adding extra layers of cultural richness to the experience.

- There are a number of restaurants and cafes located near the museum.

Museo Lapidario Maffeiano

Museo Lapidario Maffeiano is a museum in Verona, Italy, dedicated to the display of ancient stone carvings and inscriptions. It is one of the oldest public museums in Europe, founded in the 18th century by the scholar Scipione Maffei. Museo Lapidario Maffeiano is located in the heart of Verona, in the Piazza Bra, next to the Arena di Verona.

Visitors to Museo Lapidario Maffeiano can expect to see a wide variety of ancient stone carvings and inscriptions, including:

1. Roman inscriptions from the 1st to the 6th centuries AD
2. Greek inscriptions from the 5th to the 3rd centuries BC
3. Etruscan inscriptions from the 7th to the 3rd centuries BC
4. Stone sculptures from the Roman and Renaissance periods

5. The museum also has a collection of Roman coins and other artifacts.

Other necessary information for tourists

• Museo Lapidario Maffeiano is open from Tuesday to Sunday from 10:00 am to 6:00 pm. The museum is closed on Mondays.

• The cost of admission to Museo Lapidario Maffeiano is €6 for adults, €4 for seniors and students, and free for children under 6.

• Contact details: Museo Lapidario Maffeiano Piazza Bra, 28 37121 Verona, Italy Tel: +39 045 800 5847.

• Museo Lapidario Maffeiano is wheelchair accessible.

• The museum has a small gift shop.

• There are a number of restaurants and cafes located near the museum.

• The best time to visit the museum is during the shoulder season (April-May and September-October), when the crowds are smaller.

- If you are visiting during the summer months, be sure to wear comfortable shoes and a hat, as the museum can be quite hot.
- Guided tours may be available, providing a deeper understanding of the inscriptions and artifacts on display.

Museo di Storia Naturale di Verona

The Museo di Storia Naturale di Verona (Verona Natural History Museum) is a museum in Verona, Italy, located in the Palazzo Pompei, a Renaissance palace built in the 16th century. The museum houses a collection of natural history specimens, including fossils, minerals, and zoological specimens.

Visitors to the Museo di Storia Naturale di Verona can expect to see a wide variety of natural history specimens, including:

1. Fossils from the Paleozoic, Mesozoic, and Cenozoic eras, including dinosaurs, sea reptiles, and mammals

2. Minerals from all over the world

3. Zoological specimens from all over the world, including birds, fish, insects, and mammals

The museum also offers a variety of educational programs and events, including guided tours, workshops, and lectures.

Other necessary information for tourists

- The Museo di Storia Naturale di Verona is open from Tuesday to Sunday from 8:30 am to 7:30 pm. The museum is closed on Mondays.
- The cost of admission to the Museo di Storia Naturale di Verona is €4.50 for adults, €3.00 for children under 14 years old, and free for children under 6 years old.
- Contact details: Museo di Storia Naturale di Verona
Lungo Adige Porta Vittoria, 9 37122 Verona, Italy Tel: +39 045 711 0129.
- The museum is wheelchair accessible, ensuring inclusivity for all visitors.

- Photography without flash is permitted for personal use.

- Guided tours may be available, offering a deeper exploration of the museum's exhibits.

- There is a parking garage located near the museum.

- If you are visiting during the peak season (summer), it is a good idea to purchase your tickets in advance to avoid long lines.

- There are a number of restaurants and cafes located near the museum.

Activities for Solo Travelers

Verona beckons solo travelers with open arms, offering a wealth of experiences tailored for those exploring on their own. This section is your guide to discovering the city's hidden treasures, making new connections, and reveling in the liberating joy of solo exploration. Verona is your canvas for a solo adventure filled with self-discovery and unforgettable moments.

Cooking class

Verona is a great mediaeval city to take a cooking class and learn how to make some of your favorite Italian dishes.

Here are a few different cooking classes you can take in Verona:

1. Italian Risotto recipes and Pasta Cooking Class: This class is located at Via Podgora, 25, 37123 Verona VR, Italy. Contact details: +39 045 595 078.

In this class, you will learn how to make two of Italy's most popular dishes: risotto and pasta. You will learn about the different types of rice and pasta used in Italian cuisine, as well as the different cooking techniques used to make these dishes. You will also get to taste the dishes you make at the end of the class.

2. My Granny's secrets: Making pasta in the heart of Verona: This class is located at Piazza dei Signori, 28,

37121 Verona VR, Italy. Contact details: +39 347 769 7618.

In this class, you will learn how to make pasta from scratch using traditional Italian methods. You will learn about the different types of flour and water used in Italian pasta, as well as the different techniques used to knead and roll out the dough. You will also get to taste the pasta you make at the end of the class.

3. Gelato Making Class in Verona: This class is located at Vicolo Carmelitani Scalzi, 14c, 37121 Verona VR, Italy. Contact details: +39 338 102 0401.

In this class, you will learn how to make gelato, Italian ice cream. You will learn about the different types of milk and sugar used in gelato, as well as the different techniques used to churn and freeze the gelato. You will also get to taste the gelato you make at the end of the class.

Most cooking classes in Verona are small groups, so you will have plenty of personal attention from the instructor. The classes are typically hands-on, so you will get to participate in all aspects of preparing the dishes. You will also gain insights into the rich historical and cultural aspects of Italian culinary traditions.

The cost of cooking classes in Verona varies depending on the type of class, the length of the class, and the number of people in the class. However, most classes cost between €50 and €100.

Other necessary information for tourists

• Many cooking classes offer a variety of languages, so be sure to inquire about the language of the class before you book.

• Some cooking classes require you to wear an apron and safety glasses. Be sure to ask about the dress code before you book.

- Most cooking classes offer pick-up and drop-off services from your hotel. Be sure to inquire about this service before you book.

Wine tasting

1. Valpolicella Tasting - Wine & Food Tours in Verona: This tour takes you to the Valpolicella region, which is known for its Amarone, Ripasso, and Recioto wines. You will visit two wineries and sample a variety of wines. The tour also includes a traditional Italian lunch.

- Location: Via XXIV Maggio, 18/c.
- Contact: +39 349 006 7155
- Cost: The cost of the tour is €110 per person.

2. Taste Verona wine tours: This tour takes you to two wineries in the Valpolicella region. You will sample a variety of wines, including Amarone, Ripasso, and Recioto. The tour also includes a light lunch.

- Location: Via Dino Buzzati, 6.
- Contact: +39 340 244 6417

- Cost: The cost of the tour is €90 per person.

3. Pagus Wine Tours: This tour takes you to three wineries in the Valpolicella region. You will sample a variety of wines, including Amarone, Ripasso, and Recioto. The tour also includes a traditional Italian lunch.
- Location: Corso Castelvecchio, 3a.
- Contact: +39 327 796 5380
- Cost: The cost of the tour is €120 per person.

Other necessary information for tourists

- Wine tasting tours typically last for four to five hours.
- Some tours include lunch, while others do not.
- It is a good idea to book your tour in advance, especially if you are visiting during the peak season (summer).
- Most tours are in English, but some tours are also available in other languages.

Walking tour

There are many different walking tours available that can help you discover all that Verona has to offer. Here are a few of the most popular walking tours in Verona:

1. Free Walking Tour Verona: This tour is a great way to see the highlights of Verona on a budget. The tour covers all of the main attractions, including the Verona Arena, Juliet's House, and Piazza dei Signori. Contact: +39 345 188 0849

The tour is about 2 hours long and covers the main attractions of Verona. The tour is led by a local guide who will share their knowledge of the city's history and culture. This tour is free (tips are appreciated)

The tour starts at 10:30 am every day. Reservations are not required, but are recommended during the peak season.

2. Verona Highlights Walking Tour: This tour is a great option for visitors who want to learn more about the history and culture of Verona. The tour covers all of the main attractions, as well as some hidden gems. Contact, +39 045 597 311

The tour is about 2.5 hours long and covers the main attractions of Verona, as well as some hidden gems. The tour is led by a local guide who will share their knowledge of the city's history and culture.

- Cost: €20 for adults, €10 for children
- The tour starts at 10:30 am every day. Reservations are required.

3. Romeo and Juliet Walking Tour: This tour is a must-do for fans of Shakespeare's Romeo and Juliet. The tour takes you to all of the locations from the play, including Juliet's House and the Verona Arena.

The tour is about 1.5 hours long and covers all of the locations from Shakespeare's Romeo and Juliet. The tour is led by a local guide who will share their knowledge of the play and its history.

- Contact: +39 045 803 2989
- Cost: €15 for adults, €10 for children
- The tour starts at 10:30 am and 2:00 pm every day. Reservations are required.

These represent only a small selection of the numerous walking tours that Verona has to offer. With a wide array of choices available, you'll undoubtedly discover the ideal tour that aligns with your preferences and financial plans.

Biking tour

Verona is a beautiful city, perfect for exploring by bike. There are a number of different biking tours available, so you can choose one that suits your interests and fitness level.

1. Bikethecity Verona Bike Tours
- Contact: +39 333 631 5730
- Website: https://www.bikethecity.it/

2. Itinera Bike & Travel

- Contact: +39 045 222 6529
- Website: http://www.itinerabike.com/

3. Ways Tours

- Contact: +39 045 570 1561
- Website: https://waystours.com/category/visit-verona/

Biking tours in Verona typically last for 2-3 hours and cover a distance of 5-10 kilometers. You will visit some of the city's most popular tourist attractions, such as the Arena di Verona, Piazza delle Erbe, and Castelvecchio. You will also have the opportunity to learn about the city's history and culture from your experienced guide.

The cost of biking tours in Verona varies depending on the length of the tour and the company you book with. However, you can expect to pay around €25-30 per person for a 2-3 hour tour.

Other necessary information for tourists

• Ensure you wear attire and footwear that is comfortable for your excursion.

• Remember to pack a water bottle and sunscreen for your trip.

• If your visit falls during the summer season, it's advisable to commence your tour in the early morning to escape the sweltering heat.

• For those lacking confidence in their cycling abilities, there are various electric bike tour options available.

• Advance booking for your tour is highly recommended, especially if your visit aligns with the peak season.

• Don't hesitate to pose questions to your tour guide about the city and its rich history.

• Make the most of your journey by taking periodic breaks to relish the scenic views and capture some memorable photos.

• Lastly, ensure you have your camera with you to document your adventure.

• Helmets, maps, and safety instructions are provided, ensuring a secure and enjoyable biking experience.

Festivals and Events

Verona is a city that knows how to throw a party, with a vibrant calendar of festivals and events that cater to all tastes. Here are some of the top celebrations that light up the city:

1. Verona Opera Festival (Arena di Verona Opera Festival) June to September: Held in the iconic Verona Arena, this world-renowned opera festival showcases spectacular performances in a historic setting. Audiences gather under the starlit sky to be swept away by the power of opera. The festival features a variety of operas, including some of the most popular works by composers such as Verdi, Puccini, and Bizet. The performances are held in the evening and typically last for three hours. Tickets for the opera festival can be purchased online or at the box office.

Insider Tips:

• The Arena di Verona is an open-air venue, so it is important to dress appropriately for the weather.

- There are a number of restaurants and cafes located near the Arena di Verona, so you can enjoy a meal or drink before or after the performance.
- If you are staying in Verona for the Arena di Verona Opera Festival, there are a number of hotels located within walking distance of the venue.
- Bring a cushion to sit on, as the seats in the Arena di Verona are made of stone.

2. Vinitaly (April): Italy's largest wine exhibition, Vinitaly, transforms Verona into a paradise for wine enthusiasts. Sample exquisite Italian wines, attend seminars, and connect with experts in the industry. The festival is held in the Veronafiere, a trade fair complex located just outside the city center. The Verona Wine Festival is a ticketed event. Guests have the option to buy tickets either through online platforms or upon arrival at the venue. The festival features a variety of booths where visitors can sample wines from different wineries. There are also food booths, as well as cooking demonstrations and other events.

3. Tocatì - International Festival of Street Games (September): Streets and piazzas come alive with Tocatì, a celebration of traditional and contemporary street games from around the world. Visitors can join in the fun or simply enjoy the lively atmosphere.

4. Verona in Love (Verona in Amore) February: Valentine's Day takes on a special significance in Verona, the city of Romeo and Juliet. Love-themed events, from concerts to romantic dinners, fill the streets, creating a magical atmosphere.

5. Festival of the Patron Saint (Festa della Patrona) September 4th: Verona pays tribute to its patron saint, Saint Zeno, with religious processions, cultural events, and a lively fair. The highlight is the traditional candlelit procession along the Adige River.

6. Christmas Markets (Mercatini di Natale) December: The festive season comes alive with Christmas markets, where stalls brim with handcrafted gifts, seasonal treats, and holiday decorations. The markets add a touch of magic to Verona's winter landscape.

7. Verona Jazz Festival (July to August): The Verona Jazz Festival is one of the most important jazz festivals in Italy. It features a variety of jazz musicians from around the world, including both established artists and up-and-coming performers. The festival is held in a number of different venues throughout the city, including the Arena di Verona, the Teatro Romano, and the Castelvecchio. The Verona Jazz Festival is a multi-day event that features a variety of concerts, workshops, and other events. Tickets for the festival can be purchased online or at the box office.

Sporting event

Verona is not only a city of art and culture but also a hub for exhilarating sporting events. Here are some of the top athletic competitions that draw crowds and ignite the city with energy:

1. Verona Marathon (Maratona di Verona) February/March: The Verona Marathon is a premier running event that winds through the city's scenic streets and past historic landmarks. Participants, from seasoned athletes to first-time runners, come together for a day of endurance and camaraderie.

2. Giro d'Italia (May): As one of the prestigious Grand Tours of cycling, the Giro d'Italia occasionally includes Verona as a stage. Spectators line the streets to cheer on the world's top cyclists as they race through the city.

3. Arena CrossFit Games (October): The Arena CrossFit Games bring together fitness enthusiasts from around the world to compete in a series of challenging workouts. The event showcases strength, endurance, and determination in the stunning backdrop of the Verona Arena.

4. Horse Racing at the Fiera di San Zeno (November): The Fiera di San Zeno is a historic horse race that pays homage to Verona's patron saint.

Participants don period costumes and compete in a thrilling race along the city's main street.

5. Verona Volley Matches September to April (seasonal): For fans of volleyball, catching a match with the Verona Volley team at the PalaOlimpia is a must. The electrifying atmosphere and world-class talent on display make for an unforgettable sporting experience.

6. Serie A football matches: Verona Calcio plays in the Serie A, the top division of Italian football. The club plays its home matches at the Stadio Marcantonio Bentegodi.

7. Fieracavalli: Fieracavalli is an international horse fair that is held in Verona every year in October. The event features a variety of horse shows, competitions, and exhibitions.

8. Bra Verona Marathon: The Bra Verona Marathon is a marathon that is held in Verona every year in November. The race starts and finishes in the Piazza delle Erbe, and it passes through some of the city's most iconic landmarks.

Tips for Tourists:
- Check the official event websites or local listings for specific dates and ticket information.
- Arrive early, especially for popular events, to secure a good viewing spot.
- Familiarize yourself with the event's venue and any relevant transportation details to ensure a smooth experience.

Nightlife and Party

Verona is a beautiful city with a vibrant nightlife scene. There are a number of different places to go out at night in Verona, depending on your interests and budget.

Here are some of the best places to go out at night in Verona:

1. Piazza delle Erbe: Piazza delle Erbe is the main square in Verona and is a popular spot for both locals and tourists. There are a number of bars and restaurants in the square, as well as street performers and musicians.

2. Corso Porta Borsari: Corso Porta Borsari is a pedestrian street that is lined with bars and restaurants. It's a renowned location for observing people and savoring a drink.

3. Via Garibaldi: Via Garibaldi is a popular street for nightlife, and is home to a number of bars and clubs.

4. Piazza Brà: Piazza Brà is a large square that is located in the heart of Verona. It is a popular spot for both locals and tourists, and is home to a number of bars and restaurants.

5. Ponte Scaligero: Ponte Scaligero is a medieval bridge that is located in Verona. It is a popular spot for both locals and tourists, and offers stunning views of the city at night.

What kind of fun can be had in Verona at night:

● **Enjoy a drink at a bar or restaurant:** Verona has a wide variety of bars and restaurants to choose from, so you can find the perfect place to enjoy a drink and relax.

● **Go to a club:** Verona has a number of clubs that cater to different music tastes, so you can find the perfect club to dance the night away.

● **See a show:** Verona has a number of theaters and concert venues that host a variety of shows throughout the year.

● **Take a walk around the city:** Verona is a beautiful city to explore at night. Take a walk around the city center and admire the illuminated buildings and monuments.

● **Have a picnic in the park:** Verona has a number of parks that are perfect for a picnic at night. Pack a basket of food and drinks and enjoy a meal under the stars.

Verona has a vibrant nightlife scene, with a variety of clubs to choose from, depending on your music taste and budget. Here are some of the top nightclubs in Verona:

1. Dorian Gray: Dorian Gray is one of the most popular nightclubs in Verona, known for its eclectic mix of music, from hip hop and R&B to EDM and house. The club has a large dance floor and a number of bars, as well as a VIP area. Dorian Gray is located in Via Belobono, 13, Verona.

2. Berfi's Club: Berfi's Club is a smaller, more intimate club that is known for its live music performances. The club has a variety of local and international bands and DJs performing throughout the week. Berfi's Club is located in Via Scalzi, 12, Verona.

3. The Firm Club: The Firm Club is a large nightclub that is known for its big-name DJs and live performances. The club has a large dance floor and a number of bars, as well as a VIP area. The Firm Club is located in Viale dell'Industria, 24, Verona.

4. City Night Club: City Night Club is a popular nightclub that is known for its mix of commercial and underground music. The club has a large dance floor and a number of bars, as well as a VIP area. City Night Club is located in Strada Bresciana, 1, Verona.

5. Hollywood Dance Club: Hollywood Dance Club is a large nightclub that is located on the outskirts of Verona. The club is known for its big-name DJs and live performances, as well as its large dance floor and multiple bars. Hollywood Dance Club is located in Via Brescia, 200, Verona.

Other notable nightclubs in Verona include Penultimo Drink, Madigan's Pub, Scalette bistró, Grupo Sempre Se Caffè Dell'ammiraglio and Bear shop.

Shopping, Markets and Boutiques

Verona also boasts a thriving shopping scene. From quaint boutiques tucked away in charming alleys to bustling markets brimming with local wares, Verona offers a delightful array of shopping experiences. Whether you're seeking high-end fashion, artisanal crafts, or delectable culinary treasures, this city invites you on a journey of retail exploration.

1. Piazza delle Erbe Market: This vibrant market in the heart of Verona is a kaleidoscope of colors, scents, and flavors. Stroll through stalls adorned with fresh produce, local delicacies, artisanal crafts, and souvenirs. It's the perfect place to savor the essence of Verona.

Opening Hours: Monday to Sunday: 8:00 AM - 8:00 PM

2. Mercato di Porta Palio: A local favorite, this market offers a diverse range of goods, from clothing and accessories to household items and fresh produce. Immerse yourself in the authentic ambiance as you peruse the stalls.

Opening Hours: Monday to Saturday: 7:30 AM - 2:00 PM, Closed on Sundays

3. Via Mazzini Boutiques: Via Mazzini is Verona's premier shopping street, lined with a collection of high-end boutiques and designer stores. Here, you'll find the latest fashion trends, luxury accessories, and stylish footwear, making it a haven for fashion enthusiasts.

Opening Hours: 10:00 am - 7:00 pm (Monday-Saturday)

4. Antica Bottega del Vino: This historic wine boutique is a paradise for oenophiles. Explore an extensive selection of fine Italian wines and rare vintages, and even indulge in tastings paired with delectable local cheeses.

Opening Hours: Monday to Saturday: 9:00 AM - 12:00 AM, Sundays: 10:00 AM - 12:00 AM.

5. Mercato dell'Antiquariato: The Mercato dell'Antiquariato is an antiques market held on the second Sunday of every month. The market sells a variety of antiques, including furniture, paintings, and jewelry.

6. Mercato di Porta Vescovo: The Mercato di Porta Vescovo is a weekly market held on Tuesdays and Fridays. The market sells a variety of items, including clothing, accessories, and food.

Tips for Tourists:

- Remember to carry cash, as some markets may not accept card payments. However, Many of the boutiques in Verona accept credit cards.
- Bargaining is not a common practice in boutiques, but it may be acceptable in certain markets. Use your discretion.
- Be sure to bring your passport if you are planning on buying high-end items.
- The markets and boutiques in Verona are typically closed on Sundays.

Travel Itinerary Planner

CHAPTER FOUR: DAY TRIPS FROM VERONA

While Verona offers a treasure trove of experiences within its ancient walls, the surrounding region beckons with its own array of wonders. This chapter invites you to embark on enchanting day trips, each promising a unique adventure beyond Verona's city limits. From the picturesque shores of Lake Garda to the historic charm of Mantua, these destinations promise to enrich your Italian journey with new sights, flavors, and experiences.

Lake Garda

Approximately 30 kilometers (15.5 miles) from Verona, Lake Garda is a convenient day trip destination that beckons with its breathtaking beauty. Lake Garda, also known as Lago di Garda, is the largest lake in Italy and one of the most popular tourist destinations in the country. Lake Garda invites you to bask in its natural beauty and soak up its serene ambiance. With a plethora of activities to choose from, it promises a day trip from

Verona that's filled with relaxation, adventure, and unforgettable moments.

There are a few different ways to get to Lake Garda from Verona:

1. By Car: Renting a car is a flexible and convenient way to get around. The duration of the journey varies between 30 to 40 minutes, contingent on the prevailing traffic conditions.. You can take the A4 motorway or the Strada Regionale 11.

2. By Bus: Buses from Verona's Porta Nuova station run regularly to various towns along Lake Garda's shores, including Desenzano, Sirmione, and Garda. The journey typically takes around 45-60 minutes.

3. By Train: Take a train from Verona Porta Nuova to Desenzano del Garda, which is one of the main train stations on the lake. The train journey lasts approximately 20 minutes.

There are a variety of activities to do at Lake Garda, including:

1. Exploring Sirmione: Visit the charming town of Sirmione, known for its medieval castle, Roman ruins, and therapeutic hot springs. Stroll through its narrow streets and enjoy panoramic views of the lake.

2. Boat Tours: Hop on a boat tour to fully appreciate the grandeur of Lake Garda. Many operators offer scenic cruises, allowing you to admire the picturesque towns and surrounding mountains.

3. Watersports: For the adventurous, Lake Garda offers opportunities for windsurfing, sailing, and kiteboarding. Equipment rental and lessons are readily available.

4. Wine Tasting: The Lake Garda region is known for its vineyards. Consider visiting a local winery for a tasting session, sampling some of the area's finest vintages.

5. Relaxing on the Beaches: Numerous beaches and lakeside promenades offer idyllic spots for sunbathing, picnicking, and taking in the serene surroundings.

6. Visiting theme parks: There are a number of theme parks located near Lake Garda, such as Gardaland and Movieland Park. For families or thrill-seekers, Gardaland amusement park is just a stone's throw away and promises a day of excitement and entertainment.

Other necessary information for tourists

• **Ferry Services:** Regular ferries and boats connect various towns around the lake, making it easy to explore multiple locations in a day.

• Dining: Lake Garda is renowned for its fresh seafood and regional delicacies. Don't miss the opportunity to savor local flavors at lakeside restaurants.

• The best time to visit Lake Garda is during the summer months (June-September), when the weather is warm and sunny.

Soave, Wine and Castle Country

Soave offers a delightful escape from Verona, inviting visitors to immerse themselves in its rich history, picturesque landscapes, and delectable wines. With its relaxed pace and timeless beauty, this charming town promises a day trip filled with unforgettable moments. Located just 25 kilometers east of Verona, Soave is a delightful day trip destination that beckons with its enchanting medieval charm.

There are a few different ways to get from Verona to Soave:

1. By Train: There is a train from Verona Porta Nuova to Castelnuovo del Garda. From Castelnuovo del Garda, you can take a bus to Soave. The cumulative duration of the journey amounts to approximately 75 minutes.

2. By Car: A scenic 30-minute drive along the SS11 or A4/E70 will lead you from Verona to Soave, offering picturesque views along the way.

3. By bus: There is a direct bus from Verona to Soave that takes about 45 minutes. The bus departs from the Verona Porta Nuova train station.

Activities that can be done in Soave:

1. Explore the Soave Castle (Castello Scaligero): This iconic castle dominates the town's skyline and offers panoramic views of the surrounding vineyards. Delve into its history as you wander through its ancient halls.

2. Wine Tasting in Soave Vineyards: Soave is renowned for its exquisite white wines. Visit local wineries for tastings and tours, where you can savor the flavors of the region and perhaps even bring home a bottle of this liquid gold.

3. Stroll Through Soave's Historic Center: Wander the cobbled streets, where charming shops and cafes await discovery. Admire the well-preserved medieval architecture that transports you back in time.

4. Visit the Museo del Costume: Located in the Palazzo di Giustizia, this museum showcases traditional clothing and artifacts, providing insights into the cultural heritage of the region.

5. Enjoy a Leisurely Lunch: Indulge in local delicacies at one of Soave's quaint trattorias. Savor dishes like risotto, local cheeses, and homemade pasta, paired with a glass of the renowned Soave wine.

6. Visit the Soave Wine Museum: The Soave Wine Museum is located in the Soave Castle and tells the story of the Soave wine region. The museum also offers wine tastings.

Other necessary information for tourists

• Soave is renowned for its annual Festa dell'Uva (Grape Festival) in September, celebrating the grape harvest with parades, food stalls, and entertainment.

• The town is pedestrian-friendly, making it easy to explore on foot. However, comfortable footwear is recommended for navigating the cobbled streets. There is also a public bus that operates in the town center.

- It's advisable to check the opening hours of wineries and attractions in advance, as they may vary.

- Soave is a popular tourist destination, so it is best to visit during the shoulder season (May-June and September-October) to avoid the crowds.

- Soave is a family-friendly town with a number of activities for children.

- There are a number of restaurants and cafes located in Soave, so you will be spoiled for choice when it comes to food and drink.

Vicenza

Vicenza, a UNESCO World Heritage Site, is a city where art, history, and architecture converge to create a truly enchanting experience. Vicenza is also home to a number of museums and galleries. This day trip promises a journey through the masterpieces of Palladio and the rich cultural tapestry of this elegant Italian city. The distance between Verona and Vicenza is approximately 30 kilometers (18 miles). making it an easily accessible day trip by car or public transportation.

The easiest way to get to Vicenza from Verona is by train. The train journey takes approximately 25 minutes. There are frequent trains throughout the day, so you can easily find a train that fits your schedule.

A drive from Verona to Vicenza typically takes about 45 minutes via the A4/E70 motorway. It provides the freedom to explore at your preferred speed.

Here are some of the things you can do in Vicenza on a day trip from Verona:

1. Palladian Marvels: Vicenza is renowned for its architectural heritage, much of it designed by the illustrious Andrea Palladio. Don't miss the Teatro

Olimpico, Villa Capra "La Rotonda," and Palazzo Chiericati, which showcase Palladio's genius.

2. Basilica Palladiana: Climb to the top of this iconic basilica for panoramic views of Vicenza's historic center and the surrounding hills. The Basilica Palladiana is one of the most iconic buildings in Vicenza. It was designed by Andrea Palladio and is a UNESCO World Heritage Site.

3. Vicenza Cathedral (Duomo di Vicenza): Admire the stunning blend of Gothic and Romanesque architecture of this sacred edifice, which houses notable artworks and sculptures.

4. Olympic Theater (Teatro Olimpico): Step into the world of ancient drama at this marvel of Renaissance theater design. The wooden stage set is a masterpiece of perspective.

5. Visit the Palladian Villas: Vicenza is surrounded by a number of Palladian villas, which are country houses designed by Andrea Palladio. Some of the most popular villas to visit include the Villa Rotonda and the Villa Valmarana ai Nani.

6. Visit the Pinacoteca di Vicenza: The Pinacoteca di Vicenza is a museum that houses a collection of Italian paintings from the 14th to the 19th centuries.

7. Visit the Museo del Gioiello: The Museo del Gioiello is a museum dedicated to the history of jewelry. It houses a collection of jewelry from all over the world, dating from ancient times to the present day.

Additional Information:
- Vicenza's historic center is compact and best explored on foot or bicycle allowing you to soak in its architectural splendor at a leisurely pace.
- Local markets and charming shops offer opportunities to savor authentic Venetian cuisine and shop for unique souvenirs.

Here is a possible itinerary for a day trip to Vicenza from Verona:

9:00 AM: Take the train from Verona Porta Nuova station to Vicenza station. The journey takes about 30 minutes.

9:30 AM: Arrive in Vicenza and walk to the Basilica Palladiana, a UNESCO World Heritage Site. This stunning basilica was designed by Andrea Palladio, one of the most important architects of the Renaissance.

10:30 AM: After visiting the Basilica Palladiana, take a walk around the Piazza dei Signori, the heart of Vicenza's historic center. The square is surrounded by beautiful buildings, including the Palazzo Chiericati and the Palazzo del Capitaniato.

11:30 AM: For lunch, stop at one of the many restaurants in the Piazza dei Signori or in the nearby streets.

12:30 PM: After lunch, visit the Teatro Olimpico, another of Palladio's masterpieces. This unique theater was built in the 16th century and is still used for performances today.

2:00 PM: After visiting the Teatro Olimpico, take a walk through the Giardino Salvi, a beautiful public garden.

3:00 PM: If you have time, visit the Palladio Museum, which is dedicated to the life and work of Andrea Palladio.

4:00 PM: Take the train from Vicenza station back to Verona Porta Nuova station.

5:00 PM: Arrive in Verona.

This provided itinerary is merely a recommended plan, and you have the flexibility to tailor it to your specific preferences and scheduling requirements. For example, if you are interested in art, you could visit the Palazzo Chiericati Museum or the Museo Civico. If you are interested in history, you could visit the Museo del Risorgimento e dell'Età Contemporanea or the Museo Naturalistico Archeologico. And if you are traveling with children, you could visit the Parco Querini or the Città dei Bambini.

Trento

Trento, with its blend of history, natural beauty, and cultural richness, provides a perfect day trip escape from Verona. Immerse yourself in the tranquil ambiance of this Alpine gem and northern Italian province of Trentino-Alto Adige and return with memories that will last a lifetime. Trento is located approximately 98 kilometers (61 miles) north of Verona, making it an accessible and picturesque day trip destination.

The fastest way to get from Verona to Trento is by train. The journey takes about one hour. There are also regular buses that run from Verona to Trento, but the journey takes about an hour and a half.

Activities that can be done in Trento:

1. Buonconsiglio Castle (Castello del Buonconsiglio):
Explore this stunning castle complex, a testament to Trento's rich history. Admire its architecture, stroll through the courtyards, and visit the museum housed within.

2. Trento Cathedral (Cattedrale di San Vigilio):
Marvel at the Romanesque architecture of this cathedral, dedicated to Saint Vigilius. Make sure not to miss the chance to ascend the tower and enjoy breathtaking panoramic vistas of the city.

3. Museo Tridentino di Scienze Naturali: Delve into the natural history of the region at this museum. Exhibits showcase the flora, fauna, and geological wonders of the Trentino region.

4. Piazza Duomo: Relax in this charming square, surrounded by historic buildings and cafes. It's an ideal spot for people-watching and savoring local delicacies.

5. Aperitivo in Piazza Fiera: Experience the Italian tradition of aperitivo in the lively Piazza Fiera. Choose from a variety of bars and enjoy a pre-dinner drink with complimentary snacks.

6. Bike Ride along the Adige River: Rent a bike and follow the scenic Adige River bike path, offering breathtaking views of the surrounding mountains and countryside.

7. Museo Storico della Guerra del Trentino: The Museo Storico della Guerra del Trentino is a museum that is dedicated to the history of the First World War. The museum has a number of exhibits that tell the story of the war and its impact on the region.

8. Giardini di Castel Toblino: The Giardini di Castel Toblino are a beautiful botanical garden that is located on the shores of Lake Toblino. The garden is home to a variety of plants and flowers, as well as a medieval castle

Additional Information:

- **Local Cuisine:** Treat yourself to Trentino's delectable specialties, such as canederli (dumplings), polenta, and local cheeses.
- **Shopping:** Explore the boutiques and shops in the city center, offering unique crafts and local products.
- **Language:** While Italian is the official language, English is widely understood in tourist areas.
- Trento is a relatively small city, so it is easy to get around on foot or by public transportation.

Here is a possible itinerary for a day trip to Trento from Verona:

9:00 am: Take the train from Verona to Trento.

10:00 am: Arrive in Trento and head to the Duomo di Trento.

11:00 am: Visit the Museo Storico della Guerra del Trentino.

12:30 pm: Have lunch at one of the many restaurants in Piazza Duomo.

2:00 pm: Take the bus to the Giardini di Castel Toblino.

4:00 pm: Take the bus back to Trento.

5:00 pm: Visit Buonconsiglio Castle.

7:00 pm: Have dinner at one of the many restaurants in Trento.

8:30 pm: Take the train back to Verona.

Venice

Venice, with its unique waterways and timeless beauty, is an essential day trip for any visitor to Verona. Immerse yourself in the romance and history of this floating city, and let the echoes of gondoliers and the lapping of canal waters leave an indelible mark on your Italian adventure.

Venice is a beautiful city in northeastern Italy, located about 110 kilometers from Verona. It is a popular tourist destination known for its canals, gondolas, and Doge's Palace.

There are a few different ways to get to Venice from Verona:

1. By Train: The train is the fastest and most convenient way to get to Venice from Verona. The duration of the journey is approximately 75 minutes. Trains depart from Verona Porta Nuova station every 30 minutes.

2. By Car: Drive along the A4 motorway towards Venice. The journey takes about 1.5 to 2 hours, depending on traffic. However, it is important to note that parking can be difficult and expensive in Venice.

3. By bus: There are also buses that run from Verona to Venice. The duration of the journey is approximately 90 minutes. Buses depart from Verona Piazza Bra station every hour.

Activities that can be done in Venice

1. Grand Canal Cruise: Hop aboard a vaporetto (water bus) and glide along the iconic Grand Canal. Admire the splendid palaces, bustling markets, and picturesque bridges that line this famed waterway.

2. St. Mark's Basilica: Marvel at the architectural opulence of this Byzantine masterpiece. Climb the

Campanile for breathtaking views of Venice's rooftops and waterways.

3. Rialto Bridge and Market: Stroll across the Rialto Bridge, the oldest bridge spanning the Grand Canal, and explore the vibrant Rialto Market, brimming with fresh produce and Venetian specialties.

4. Gondola Ride: Indulge in a quintessential Venetian experience with a gondola ride. Drift along the narrow canals, taking in the romance and charm of this enchanting city.

5. Piazza San Marco: Wander around the renowned St. Mark's Square, soak in the lively atmosphere, and perhaps enjoy a coffee at one of the elegant cafes.

6. Murano and Burano Islands: Consider taking a short boat trip to these nearby islands. Murano is renowned for its glass-blowing artisans, while Burano enchants with its colorful houses and lacemaking tradition.

7. Get lost in the maze of canals: Venice is a city of over 100 islands and is connected by a maze of canals. Get lost in the canals and explore the city at your own pace.

8. Visit Doge's Palace: Doge's Palace was the residence of the Doge of Venice, the supreme ruler of the Republic of Venice. It is now a museum and one of the most popular tourist attractions in Venice.

Additional Information:

- **Vaporetto Tickets:** Consider purchasing a Venice Card, which provides unlimited travel on the city's water transportation system for a specified duration.
- **Dress Comfortably:** Venice is a city best explored on foot, so wear comfortable shoes for walking along its charming streets and bridges.
- **Check Return Transport:** Be mindful of the last train or bus back to Verona to ensure a smooth return journey.

Here is a possible itinerary for a day trip to Venice from Verona:

9:00 AM: Take the train from Verona Porta Nuova station to Venice Santa Lucia station.

10:15 AM: Arrive in Venice and take a gondola ride to Doge's Palace.

11:30 AM: Visit Doge's Palace.

1:00 PM: Have lunch at one of the many restaurants near Doge's Palace.

2:00 PM: Visit St. Mark's Basilica.

3:00 PM: Cross the Rialto Bridge and explore the maze of canals.

5:00 PM: Take a break for coffee or gelato at one of the many cafes in Venice.

6:00 PM: Take the train from Venice Santa Lucia station back to Verona Porta Nuova station.

7:15 PM: Arrive in Verona.

This provided itinerary is merely a recommended plan, and you have the flexibility to tailor it to your specific preferences and scheduling requirements. For example, if you are interested in art, you could visit the Peggy

Guggenheim Collection or the Gallerie dell'Accademia. If you are interested in history, you could visit the Correr Museum or the Naval History Museum. And if you are traveling with children, you could visit the Natural History Museum or the Lido di Venezia beach.

Travel Itinerary Planner

CHAPTER FIVE: ESSENTIAL TRAVEL INFORMATION

Before you embark on your Verona adventure, it's crucial to have a solid grasp of the practicalities. This chapter is your compass, providing a wealth of essential information to ensure your trip is as smooth as a gondola ride through Venetian canals. From navigating local transportation to understanding currency, we've got you covered.

Getting Around Verona, Transportation Guide

Verona is a relatively small city, and it is easy to get around on foot or by bicycle. However, there is also a public transportation system that includes buses and taxis. The public transportation system in Verona is operated by ATV (Azienda Trasporti Verona). ATV offers a variety of bus routes that connect all parts of the city. You can purchase bus tickets at newsstands, tobacco shops, and vending machines at the bus stops.

Taxis: Taxis are also available in Verona. You have the option to either flag down a taxi on the roadside or contact a taxi service provider for a ride. Taxi fares are regulated by the city of Verona.

If you're looking to experience the convenience of door-to-door transportation within Verona, you can rely on the city's taxi services. Taxis in Verona are readily accessible and can be found at designated taxi ranks situated throughout the city. These locations include the train station, Piazza Bra, and Piazza delle Erbe.

For those who require a taxi on the same day, it is advisable to make a reservation at least one hour in advance. Alternatively, you can ask your hotel to arrange a taxi for you, as taxis are typically available on short notice for your convenience.

Useful Tips for Taking Taxis in Verona

1. Pricing Variations: Taxis in Verona tend to be more expensive during the evenings and at night due to regulatory factors.

2. Meter Charges: The taxi meter starts running when the driver departs to pick you up. Therefore, when you enter the taxi, you'll notice an initial charge on the meter.

3. Safety Measures: Just like in any other location, it's important to ensure that the taxi you enter has a working meter that is actively being used.

4. Fixed Fare Taxis: Verona has fixed-rate taxis for routes to the airport and specific destinations. Before hiring a taxi, make sure you are aware of the cost. You can obtain this information from your hotel's reception or inquire with the taxi company during your initial contact.

5. Navigating the Exclusion Zone (ZTL): Verona's historical center, including areas around notable attractions like Piazza Bra and Verona Porta Nuova, is part of the ZTL (Zona a Traffico Limitato). The ZTL is established to maintain the city's UNESCO World Heritage status and reduce pollution by restricting unauthorized vehicles during certain hours.

The timing of these restrictions can vary, so it's crucial to check the specific hours for your visit. ZTL areas are clearly marked with signs, usually featuring a white circle with a red border, indicating the operational hours of the restriction. Unauthorized entry into the ZTL can result in substantial fines, as cameras monitor these zones.

Certain vehicles, such as those of residents or delivery vehicles, may be exempt from the restrictions. If your accommodation is within the ZTL, your hotel can provide you with a permit or guide you on how to obtain one. Due to these restrictions, many visitors opt to park outside the ZTL in paid or free parking areas and explore the central areas using public transportation, bicycles, or by walking. This allows you to immerse yourself in the city's ambiance without the stress of navigating the restricted zones.

In Verona, taxis offer a convenient way to explore the city. Keep these tips in mind and familiarize yourself with the designated taxi stands around town for a hassle-free experience.

2. Bicycles: Verona is a bike-friendly city, and there are a number of bicycle rental shops located throughout the city. You also have the option to hire a bicycle directly from your hotel. The city offers a bike-sharing program known as Verona Bike, which provides convenient stations located centrally at Piazza Bra and the Castelvecchio Museum.

Alternatively, if you're interested in gaining a deeper understanding of this historic town while getting a great orientation, you can consider participating in a guided bike tour. This tour will not only provide you with a local perspective of the city but also give you the chance to explore its rich history. You'll have the opportunity to pedal your way to the heart of the city, crossing the River Adige, and visit attractions such as the Basilica of San Zeno and the charming Art Nouveau villas in the Borgo Trento neighbourhood, one of Verona's most picturesque areas. Enjoy the scenic cycling routes with minimal traffic, making it easy to pause for photo opportunities along the way.

3. Buses: Operated by ATV (Azienda Trasporti Verona), Verona's extensive bus network provides convenient transportation options for both local residents and tourists within the city and its surrounding areas. These distinctive green ATV buses operate daily, offering a reliable and frequent service that caters to the needs of travelers. Verona boasts an abundance of bus stops, ensuring accessibility throughout the day, especially in the city center, residential neighbourhoods, and near the Verona Porta Nuova train station.

It's important to note that schedules and bus routes vary on Sundays, bank holidays, and during nighttime hours. The primary bus terminal in Verona is situated directly in front of the Verona Porta Nuova train station, serving as a hub for city buses connecting various neighbourhoods and providing transportation to the surrounding provinces, spanning from the northern shores of Lake Garda to the southern reaches of the Verona district. To enhance your travel experience, consider downloading the dedicated bus route and timetable app for added convenience.

Train: Verona's railway services offer an additional means of public transportation for commuters and travelers. The city benefits from two primary railway stations, namely Porta Nuova and Porta Vescovo.

Verona Porta Nuova serves as a bustling transportation hub at the heart of Italy. It plays a pivotal role as a crossroads, connecting the north-south Brenner Railway, which serves as a vital link between Austria and Bologna, with the east-west Milan-Venice railway. This intersection of major rail lines facilitates seamless connectivity.

The Verona Porta Nuova train station provides swift connections to other major cities like Milan, Florence, and Venice, all reachable in under two hours through high-speed train services. This station is particularly convenient for those planning day trips or traveling to and from the city.

Situated in the eastern part of the city, Verona Porta Vescovo is located at the charming Piazzale XXV Aprile. Established in 1847, this station holds historical significance along the Milan-Venice railway route, making it an essential stop for travelers in the Veneto region of northern Italy. Inside Porta Vescovo, you can find a cozy magazine stall and a delightful café, which also serves as a ticketing center. Porta Vescovo is known for being the quieter of Verona's two railway stations. It serves as the starting point for various train services, including:

- Express services (Regionale Veloce), which provide swift connections between Verona, Vicenza, Padua, and Venice.
- Regional services (Treno regionale) that seamlessly link Verona with these charming cities.

Porta Vescovo is conveniently located within a 30-minute walk, covering approximately 1.5 kilometers, or a quick 10-minute bus ride from the iconic Arena di Verona.

The Verona Card: A tourist pass in Verona offers unlimited access to the city's local buses at no extra cost. You can choose between a 24-hour or 48-hour pass, depending on your preference. Additionally, this pass provides entry to select attractions for the chosen duration, resulting in significant cost savings for travelers who plan to use public transportation extensively during their visit.

It's worth noting that the hop-on hop-off bus service within the city can be considered a great value when it comes to transportation. While you do need to purchase a ticket for a set period of either 24 or 48 hours, this one-time expense allows you the freedom to ride the red tourist bus as many times as you like. This single purchase not only covers the cost of a few local bus rides but also provides added benefits such as well-planned routes that highlight the city's top attractions.

Given these advantages, it's easy to see why some people view the transportation offered by the hop-on hop-off service as a practically 'free' and irresistible offer.

There are a few places where you can buy a Verona Card.

- **Tourist Information Office:** The Tourist Information Office is located in Piazza Bra, the main square in Verona. You can purchase a Verona Card at the counter during the office's opening hours.

- **Arena di Verona:** You can also purchase a Verona Card at the ticket office of the Arena di Verona, the city's Roman amphitheater. The ticket office is open daily from 10:00 AM to 4:00 PM.

- **Castelvecchio Museum:** The Castelvecchio Museum is another place where you can purchase a Verona Card.

The museum is open from Tuesday to Sunday from 8:30 AM to 7:00 PM.

- **Online:** You can also purchase a Verona Card online. Simply visit the Verona Card website and select the type of card you want and the number of days you want it to be valid for. You can then pay for your card with a credit or debit card. The Verona Card website is https://www.visitverona.it/en/verona-card/

Once you have purchased your Verona Card, you will need to activate it at one of the following locations: Tourist Information Office, Arena di Verona, Castelvecchio Museum and Any of the other participating attractions.

Once your card is activated, you can start using it to enjoy free admission to Verona's top attractions and unlimited use of public transportation.

On Foot: Verona's tales can be found not only in its renowned landmarks but also in the undiscovered corners waiting to be explored. To truly experience the city's essence, from the bustling Piazza Bra to the tranquil alleyways, there's no better way than on foot. With each step, you can discover hidden treasures such as the lush Giusti Park with its intricate gardens or the peaceful allure of San Zeno's basilica, away from the usual tourist crowds.

I embarked on a lot of walking during my time in Verona. Walking in this city is more than just a mode of transportation; it's a journey through history. The city's heart, especially in vibrant spaces like Piazza Bra, comes to life most vividly when explored on foot.

While wandering, you may chance upon charming cafes offering Veronese delicacies, turning your exploration into a delightful experience for both your taste buds and your spirit.

The Hop-On Hop-Off Red Bus: Discovering Verona aboard the open-top red bus is an enjoyable and convenient way to immerse yourself in the historic charm of this medieval city. Embrace the flexibility of the open-top red bus, which seamlessly complements your exploration by foot. The bus has been thoughtfully designed, offering two distinct routes that showcase Verona's most prominent attractions, ensuring you won't miss any of the UNESCO World Heritage sites in this city.

Should you wish to delve deeper into the stories of specific landmarks such as Piazza Bra or Verona Porta Nuova, it's a breeze! Just disembark at your leisure, follow your curiosity, and when you're ready, rejoin the tour from a designated stop to continue your Veronese adventure.

Explore Verona at your own pace, and enhance your experience with a multilingual audio guide that narrates the rich history and culture of Verona. Whether you're visiting for a day or two, you can select between 24-hour and 48-hour tickets to match your preferred pace of exploration.

What To Eat, Places To Eat

Verona is a city where culinary delights flourish around every corner. From cozy osterias serving traditional recipes to chic bistros offering modern interpretations, the dining scene here is a feast for the senses. This section is your passport to the gastronomic wonders of Verona. Let's explore the must-try dishes, the best places to savor them, and the hidden gems that promise to tantalize your taste buds.

Veronese Delights

Verona's culinary heritage is a tapestry of flavors, rich and diverse, with each dish telling a story of tradition and local pride. Here are some Veronese delights that should not be missed:

1. Risotto all'Amarone: A marriage of creamy Arborio rice and the robust flavors of Amarone wine, this dish is a testament to Verona's renowned wine-making prowess.

2. Risotto with Radicchio di Verona: The bitterness of radicchio meets the creaminess of risotto, creating a symphony of taste that captures the essence of the region.

3. Pastissada de Caval: This hearty stew of horse meat slow-cooked in red wine and spices is a testament to Verona's rustic culinary traditions.

4. Bigoli con l'Anatra: Thick, hand-rolled pasta is lavishly dressed in a rich duck ragù, offering a taste of true Veronese comfort.

5. Polenta e Osei: A dessert that resembles a playful nest, made from buttery polenta and adorned with tiny marzipan birds, celebrating Verona's agricultural roots.

6. Gnocchi di Susine: These plum-stuffed potato dumplings are a sweet surprise, showcasing the region's affinity for simple, yet delightful, desserts.

7. Amarone della Valpolicella: This world-renowned red wine, produced from dried grapes, is the jewel in Verona's oenological crown.

8. Ripasso della Valpolicella: A red wine born from the re-fermentation of Valpolicella wine on the lees of Amarone, resulting in a complex and deeply flavorful experience.

Sweet Temptations: Gelato, Pandoro, and More

Verona's culinary landscape isn't just about savory delights; it's also a haven for those with a sweet tooth. Indulge in these delectable treats that are sure to satisfy your cravings:

1. Gelato: A quintessential Italian experience, gelato in Verona is a delight for the senses. From creamy stracciatella to tangy lemon, the city's gelaterias offer a kaleidoscope of flavors.

2. Pandoro: This golden, star-shaped cake is a Christmas tradition in Verona. Its soft, buttery texture and dusting of powdered sugar make it a heavenly treat during the holiday season.

3. Tiramisù: Tiramisu is a traditional Italian dessert made with ladyfingers dipped in coffee, layered with a whipped mixture of eggs, sugar, and mascarpone cheese, flavored with cocoa. This decadent and delicious dessert is ideal for celebrating special moments.

4. Fregolotta: This crumbly almond tart is a local favorite, offering a perfect balance of sweet and nutty flavors. It is a delightful combination with a cup of espresso.

5. Amaretti: These chewy almond cookies are a delightful treat, often enjoyed with a glass of wine or a cup of coffee. Their slightly crunchy exterior gives way to a soft, flavorful center.

6. Baci di Giulietta: Named after Verona's most famous resident, Juliet, these chocolate kisses are filled with hazelnut cream and make for a sweet souvenir.

7. Romeo's Kisses (Baci di Romeo): A playful twist on the Baci di Giulietta, these hazelnut-filled chocolates are named after Romeo, adding a touch of romance to your confectionery experience.

8. Risotto ala Negrar: While typically a savory dish, this Veronese specialty combines the creaminess of risotto with the sweetness of Amarone wine and cherries for a unique dessert.

These sweet temptations are an integral part of Verona's culinary heritage. Whether enjoyed as an afternoon treat or a decadent finale to a meal, they offer a taste of the city's rich and diverse dessert culture. So, don't resist the allure of these sweet creations—indulge and savor every bite.

Osterias and Trattorias

The city has a number of osterias and trattorias, which are small, family-run restaurants that serve traditional Italian cuisine. Here are a few of the best osterias and trattorias in Verona:

1. Osteria al Duca: Osteria al Duca is known for its traditional Veronese dishes, such as risotto all'Amarone, pastissada de caval, and gnocchi de malga. If you are craving some nice local wine, the restaurant also has a wide variety of wines from the region.

- Location: Via Arche Scaligere, 2, 37121 Verona VR, Italy
- Price range per dish: 10-20 euros
- Contact: +39 045 594474

2. Osteria da Ugo: Osteria da Ugo is another great place to try traditional Veronese cuisine. The restaurant has a wide variety of dishes to choose from, including pasta, meat, fish, and vegetables. If you are craving some nice local wine, the restaurant also has a wide variety of wines from the region.

- Location: Vicolo Dietro Sant'Andrea, 1/b, 37121 Verona VR, Italy
- Price range per dish: 12-25 euros
- Contact: +39 045 594400

3. Trattoria alla Vecchia Verona: Trattoria alla Vecchia Verona is a popular restaurant that serves both traditional and modern Italian cuisine. The restaurant has a wide variety of dishes to choose from, including pasta, meat, fish, and pizza. If you are craving some nice local wine, the restaurant also has a wide variety of wines from the region.

- Location: Via Mazzini, 8, 37121 Verona VR, Italy
- Price range per dish: 10-20 euros

4. Trattoria Sottoriva: Trattoria Sottoriva is a traditional trattoria that serves classic Italian dishes. The restaurant is known for its fresh pasta and seafood dishes. If you'd like to have some nice local wine, the restaurant also has a wide variety of wines from the region.

- Location: Piazza delle Erbe, 16/17, 37121 Verona VR, Italy
- Price range per dish: 10-20 euros
- Contact: +39 045 8005179

5. Trattoria Osteria Al Duomo: Trattoria Osteria Al Duomo is a popular restaurant that serves both traditional and modern Italian cuisine. The restaurant has a wide variety of dishes to choose from, including pasta, meat, fish, and pizza. If you'd like to have some nice local wine, the restaurant also has a wide variety of wines from the region.

- Location: Via Duomo, 7, 37121 Verona VR, Italy
- Price range per dish: 10-20 euros

6. Trattoria Papa e Cicia: Trattoria Papa e Cicia serves traditional Veronese cuisine, including dishes such as gnocchi de malga, risotto all'Amarone, and pastissada de caval.

- Address: Via Garibaldi, 17, 37121 Verona VR, Italy

- Price range: Prices range from €10 to €20 per dish.
- Contact: +39 045 8002994

Bars and Cafe

1. Bar Caffe Borsari: Bar Caffe Borsari is a popular spot for both locals and tourists. It is located in the heart of Verona, in Piazza delle Erbe, the main square. The bar has a large outdoor terrace, where you can enjoy your drink and people-watch. Bar Caffe Borsari is known for its excellent cocktails and its wide selection of wines and beers.

- Location: Piazza delle Erbe, Verona, Italy.
- Kind of drinks: A wide range of cocktails, wines, and beers.
- Price range: (approx. €10-15 per drink)
- Contact details: +39 045 800 4334

2. Caffe al Teatro: Caffe al Teatro is a historic cafe located in Piazza Bra, next to the Arena di Verona. The cafe has been in business since 1880 and has been patronized by famous writers and artists such as Ernest

Hemingway and Gabriele D'Annunzio. Caffe al Teatro is a great place to relax and enjoy a cup of coffee or a cocktail while watching the world go by.

- Location: Piazza Bra, 12, Verona, Italy.
- Kind of drinks: A wide range of coffees, teas, and cocktails.
- Price range: (€5-10 per drink)
- Contact details: +39 045 800 2664

3. Caffe Mazzanti: Caffe Mazzanti is a traditional Italian cafe located on Corso Porta Borsari, one of the main shopping streets in Verona. The cafe is known for its excellent coffee and its delicious pastries. Caffe Mazzanti is a great place to stop for a quick pick-me-up or to enjoy a leisurely breakfast or afternoon snack.

- Location: Corso Porta Borsari, 19, Verona, Italy.
- Kind of drinks: A wide range of coffees, teas, and pastries.
- Price range: (€3-5 per drink)
- Contact details: +39 045 800 0525

4. Osteria Enoteca Il Bergamasco: Osteria Enoteca Il Bergamasco is a wine bar located in the historic center of Verona. The bar has a wide selection of Italian wines, as well as beers and cocktails. Osteria Enoteca Il Bergamasco is a great place to sample some of the best wines that Italy has to offer.

- Location: Via Stella, 6, Verona, Italy.
- Kind of drinks: A wide range of wines, beers, and cocktails.
- Price range: (€5-10 per drink)
- Contact details: +39 045 595582

5. Bar al Ponte: Bar al Ponte is a popular spot for both locals and tourists. It is located on the Ponte Scaligero, a medieval bridge that is one of the most iconic landmarks in Verona. The bar has a large outdoor terrace, where you can enjoy your drink and take in the stunning views of the city. Bar al Ponte is known for its excellent cocktails and its wide selection of wines and beers.

- Location: Ponte Scaligero, Verona, Italy.
- Kind of drinks: A wide range of cocktails, wines, and beers.

- Price range: (approx. €10-15 per drink)
- Contact details: +39 045 595077

Where To Stay in Verona

The best areas to stay in Verona depend on your interests and budget. So also, choosing the right neighbourhood in Verona can greatly enhance your experience in this charming city. Here are some of the best areas to consider for your stay:

1. Centro Storico (Historic Center): The Centro Storico is the heart of Verona and is home to the city's most popular tourist attractions, including the Arena di Verona, the Piazza delle Erbe, and the Juliet's House. The area is teeming with dining establishments, pubs, and retail stores. It has an excellent proximity to top attractions and you can find budget-friendly, mid range and luxury hotels in the area.

2. Borgo Trento: Borgo Trento is a quiet residential neighbourhood located just outside of the city center. It is a good option for families or travelers who are looking for a more relaxed atmosphere. The area is home to several universities and has a good selection of restaurants and cafes. It has a good proximity to top attractions and you can find different categories of hotels here.

3. Porta Nuova: Porta Nuova is a modern neighbourhood located near the train station. It is a good option for travelers who are looking for a convenient location. The area is home to several shopping malls and office buildings, as well as a number of hotels and restaurants.

4. Veronetta: Veronetta is a neighbourhood located on the other side of the Adige River from the city center. It is a more affordable option than the Centro Storico, but it is still close to many of the city's attractions. The area is home to the Basilica of San Zeno and the Castelvecchio Museum.

5. San Zeno: San Zeno is a neighbourhood located on the outskirts of Verona. It is a good option for travelers who are looking for a quiet and peaceful place to stay. The area is home to the Basilica of San Zeno and several other historical landmarks.

Recommended Hotels

Here are 3 strategically positioned luxury hotels in Verona that has easy access to top attractions, with their locations, price per night, and contact details:

1. Due Torri Hotel: The Due Torri Hotel is a 5-star hotel located in the heart of Verona, just steps from the Piazza delle Erbe and the Juliet's House. The hotel offers stunning views of the city from its rooftop terrace and restaurant. The Due Torri Hotel is also home to a spa and wellness center, where guests can relax and rejuvenate after a long day of sightseeing.

- Location: Piazza Sant'Anastasia, 4, 37121 Verona VR, Italy.
- Price per night: Starting at €300

- Contact details: +39 045 595044

2. Hotel Giulietta e Romeo: The Hotel Giulietta e Romeo is a 4-star hotel located in the historic center of Verona, just a short walk from the Arena di Verona and the Juliet's House. The hotel is housed in a 14th-century building and offers a variety of amenities, including a swimming pool, a fitness center, and a spa.
- Location: Via Arche Scaligere, 14, 37121 Verona VR, Italy.
- Price per night: Starting at €250
- Contact details: +39 045 8030880

3. Hotel Accademia: The Hotel Accademia is a 4-star hotel located in the historic center of Verona, just a short walk from the Piazza delle Erbe and the Juliet's House. The hotel is housed in a 16th-century building and offers a variety of amenities, including a swimming pool, a fitness center, and a sauna.
- Location: Via Scala, 12, 37121 Verona VR, Italy.
- Price per night: Starting at €200
- Contact details: +39 045 596222

All three of these hotels are strategically positioned near top attractions and offer easy access to public transportation. They also offer a variety of amenities and services that will make your stay in Verona as enjoyable as possible.

Here are 3 strategically positioned low-budget hotels in Verona that have easy access to top attractions:

1. Hotel Aurora: Hotel Aurora is a budget-friendly hotel located in the heart of Verona, just a short walk from the Arena di Verona and other top attractions. The hotel offers clean and comfortable rooms, as well as a variety of amenities, including a free breakfast buffet and a 24-hour front desk.

- Location: Via Carlo Cattaneo, 8, 37121 Verona VR, Italy
- Price per night: Starting at €50
- Contact details: +39 045 595576

2. Hotel Scalzi: Hotel Scalzi is another great budget-friendly option in Verona. The hotel is located in the historic center of the city, just a few steps from the Piazza delle Erbe and Juliet's House. Hotel Scalzi offers basic but clean and comfortable rooms, as well as a free breakfast buffet.

- Location: Via Scalzi, 25, 37121 Verona VR, Italy
- Price per night: Starting at €45
- Contact details: +39 045 8005009

3. Hotel Montemezzi: Hotel Montemezzi is a modern budget hotel located near the train station and the Porta Nuova bus terminal. The hotel offers clean and comfortable rooms, as well as a variety of amenities, including a free breakfast buffet and a 24-hour front desk.

- Location: Corso Porta Nuova, 47, 37121 Verona VR, Italy
- Price per night: Starting at €55
- Contact details: +39 045 595944

All of these hotels are strategically positioned within walking distance of Verona's top attractions, making them ideal for budget-minded travelers who want to explore the city on foot.

Budgeting and Money Saving Tips

As a financial expert and travel enthusiast who has visited Verona on several occasions for vacation, here are some invaluable budgeting and money-saving tips:

1. Plan your trip in advance: The earlier you start planning your trip, the more time you will have to find the best deals on flights, accommodation, and activities. You can also use this time to research free or low-cost things to do in Verona.

2. Consider traveling during the off-season: Verona is a popular tourist destination year-round, but prices tend to be lower during the off-season (November-March). If you can be flexible with your travel dates, you can save a significant amount of money on your trip.

3. Book your flights and accommodation in advance: Once you have decided on your travel dates, book your flights and accommodation as soon as possible. The closer you get to your travel date, the more expensive prices are likely to be.

4. Stay in a hostel or guesthouse: Hostels and guesthouses are a great way to save money on accommodation, especially if you are traveling solo or with a group of friends. Many hostels offer private rooms in addition to dorm beds, so you can find an option that fits your budget and comfort level.

5. Eat at local restaurants: Avoid eating at tourist traps, which are often overpriced and serve mediocre food. Instead, opt for eating at local restaurants, where you can find delicious and authentic Veronese cuisine at reasonable prices.

6. Take advantage of free activities: There are many free things to do in Verona, such as visiting the Piazza delle Erbe, Juliet's House, and the Castelvecchio

Museum. You can also take a free walking tour of the city to learn about its history and culture.

7. Purchase a Verona Card: The Verona Card is a pass that gives you free admission to many of the city's top attractions, including the Arena di Verona and the Castelvecchio Museum. You can also use the Verona Card to get unlimited use of public transportation.

8. Cook your own meals: If you are staying in a hostel or guesthouse that has a kitchen, you can save money by cooking your own meals. You can purchase groceries at local supermarkets and farmers markets.

9. Walk or take public transportation: Verona is a relatively small city, so it is easy to get around on foot or by public transportation. This will save you money on transportation costs, such as taxi fares and car rentals.

10. Take advantage of discounts: Many attractions and restaurants offer discounts to students, seniors, and groups. Be sure to ask about discounts before you purchase tickets or order your food.

11. Use a travel credit card: Many travel credit cards offer rewards such as points or miles that can be redeemed for travel expenses. You can also earn cash back on your purchases, which can be used to offset the cost of your trip.

12. Negotiate prices: It is common to negotiate prices for souvenirs and other goods in Verona. Don't be afraid to haggle with the vendors to get a better deal.

13. Free Wi-Fi and Communication Apps: Save on international data charges by using free Wi-Fi available in most cafes and using communication apps for calls and messages.

By following these tips, you can save money on your Verona vacation without sacrificing your enjoyment. With a little planning, you can have a wonderful and affordable trip to this beautiful city.

Language and Communication

Navigating a foreign city can be a breeze with a little linguistic preparation. Here's everything you need to know about language and communication in Verona:

1. Official Language: Italian is the official language of Verona. While English is widely spoken in tourist areas, it's always appreciated when visitors make an effort to speak some Italian.

2. Common Phrases: Learning a few basic Italian phrases can go a long way. "Buongiorno" (Good morning), "Grazie" (Thank you), and "Per favore" (Please) are excellent starting points.

3. Tourist Information Centers: Verona has several tourist information centers where you can find multilingual staff ready to assist with maps, directions, and general information.

4. Maps and Translation Apps: I always recommend using a language app to learn any language you want to learn. Carry a map or use translation apps on your phone to help with navigation. Apps like Google Translate can be invaluable for translating signs and menus.

5. English in Tourist Areas: In major tourist spots, hotels, restaurants, and shops often have English-speaking staff. However, venturing into more local areas may require a bit more Italian.

6. Menus and Food Labels: Most restaurants in tourist areas provide menus in English, but it's always fun to try reading the Italian version. Don't hesitate to ask waitstaff for clarification.

7. Transportation: Transportation signs, schedules, and announcements at train stations and bus stops are usually in Italian and English.

8. Emergency Numbers: In case of an emergency, dial 112 for assistance. Operators generally speak English, but it's always helpful to know basic Italian for clear communication.

9. Politeness Goes a Long Way: Italians appreciate it when visitors make an effort to use basic Italian phrases. Even if you stumble a bit, your attempts will be warmly received.

10. Cultural Respect: Italians are generally very warm and friendly. Remember to use polite expressions, and it's customary to greet people with a handshake or a kiss on both cheeks.

11. Language Schools and Classes: If you're interested in delving deeper into the language, consider enrolling in a local language school or taking a class while in Verona.

Staying Safe, Healthy and Smart in Verona

Ensuring your well-being and making informed choices while exploring Verona is paramount. Here are some invaluable tips to help you stay safe, healthy, and savvy during your visit:

Safety Measures:

1. Secure Your Belongings: Keep a close eye on your belongings, especially in crowded areas and tourist spots. Consider using anti-theft backpacks or pouches.

2. Use Reputable Transportation: Opt for licensed and reputable taxi services or ride-sharing apps. Be cautious when hailing unmarked vehicles.

3. Stay Informed About Local Events: Check for any local events, demonstrations, or festivals that might affect your plans. Stay clear of large crowds if you're uncomfortable.

4. Emergency Numbers: Know the local emergency numbers, including 112 for general emergencies and 113 for police assistance.

Here are some useful contacts and emergency numbers in Verona:

Emergency numbers

- 112 - National emergency number (police, ambulance, firefighters)
- 118 - Ambulance
- 115 - Fire department
- 113 - Police

Useful contacts

- Tourist Information Office: Piazza Bra, 28, 37121 Verona VR, Italy; +39 045 595020
- Verona City Council: Piazza dei Signori, 1, 37121 Verona VR, Italy; +39 045 8077611
- Verona Police Department: Via Carlo Cattaneo, 15, 37121 Verona VR, Italy; +39 045 8061111

5. Stay In Well-Lit Areas at Night: If you're out at night, stick to well-lit and populated areas. Avoid dimly lit streets and alleyways.

Healthy Tips:

1. Stay Hydrated: Verona can get warm, especially in the summer. Carry a reusable water bottle and stay hydrated, especially when exploring on foot.

2. Eat Fresh and Balanced Meals: Enjoy the local cuisine, but balance it with fresh fruits and vegetables. Seek out local markets for healthy snack options.

3. Sun Protection: Safeguard your skin from the sun's rays by utilizing sunscreen, a hat, and sunglasses as protective measures. Seek shade during peak hours to avoid overheating.

4. Comfortable Footwear: Wear comfortable and supportive shoes for exploring. You'll likely be doing a lot of walking, so take care of your feet.

5. First Aid Kit: Carry a basic first aid kit with essentials like band-aids, pain relievers, and any personal medications you may need.

6. Be careful when eating street food, and only eat from reputable vendors.

Smart Tips:

1. Local SIM Card or Portable Wi-Fi: Consider getting a local SIM card or portable Wi-Fi device for internet access. It will be handy for navigation and staying connected.

2. Use Reputable Guides and Services: When booking tours or services, choose reputable and licensed operators to ensure your experiences are safe and enjoyable.

3. Stay Informed About Local Laws: Familiarize yourself with local laws and customs to ensure you're respecting the culture and staying within legal boundaries.

4. Be careful when using public transportation: Crowded buses and trains are a prime target for pickpockets. Ensure your personal items are securely in your possession and be vigilant regarding your environment.

5. Be careful when crossing the street: Verona drivers can be aggressive, so be sure to look both ways before crossing the street.

6. Be careful when using ATMs: ATMs are a common target for thieves. Use ATMs that are located in well-lit areas and avoid using ATMs at night.

7. Be careful when buying souvenirs: There are many vendors who sell counterfeit souvenirs in Verona. Be sure to inspect any souvenirs before you buy them to make sure they are authentic.

Etiquette and Customs

Verona is a beautiful city with a rich culture and history. Here are some etiquette and customs that tourists should be aware of when visiting Verona:

1. Greetings: Italians are generally very friendly and welcoming. When greeting someone, it is customary to shake their hand and say "buongiorno" (good morning), "buonasera" (good evening), or "buonanotte" (good night). If you are close to the person, you may also kiss them on both cheeks.

2. Dress code: Italians often display a penchant for dressing elegantly when out in public. Dressing in a respectful manner is essential, particularly when visiting religious sites. It is advisable to refrain from wearing shorts, tank tops, or any attire that may be considered overly revealing.

3. Dining: Italians take their food very seriously. When dining at a restaurant, it is customary to finish all of your food. If you are unable to finish your food, you can politely ask the waiter for a "doggy bag" (sacchetto per il cane).

4. Tipping: Tipping is not mandatory in Italy, but it is customary to tip waiters and waitresses 10-15% of the bill. You can also tip taxi drivers and bellhops a few euros.

5. Public transportation: When taking public transportation, it is customary to give up your seat for the elderly, pregnant women, and disabled people. It is also important to be quiet and respectful of other passengers.

6. Noise: Italians tend to be quite vocal, but it is important to be respectful of others, especially when in public places.

6. Queuing: Italians are generally very good at queuing, but there may be exceptions in crowded areas. Be sure to respect the queue and don't cut in line.

7. Smoking: Smoking is prohibited in most public places in Italy, including restaurants, bars, and museums.

8. Photography: It is generally okay to take photographs in Verona, but be sure to ask permission before taking photographs of people.

9. Religion: Italy is a predominantly Catholic country. If you are visiting a religious site, be sure to dress appropriately and be respectful of the worshippers.

Useful Apps and Websites

Here are some useful apps and websites for a seamless Verona travel:

Verona travel websites
- Verona Tourism: https://www.visitverona.it/en
- Verona Airport: https://www.aeroportoverona.it/en/
- Verona Arena: https://ticketsarenaverona.com/

Verona maps
- Google Maps: https://maps.google.com/
- Citymapper: https://citymapper.com/?lang=en
- Maps.me: https://maps.me/

Verona weather forecast

- AccuWeather: https://www.accuweather.com/
- The Weather Channel: https://weather.com/
- Weather Underground: https://www.wunderground.com/

Currency converter

- XE Currency Converter: https://www.xe.com/
- Google Currency Converter: https://fx-rate.net/calculator/
- Universal Currency Converter: http://www.convertmymoney.com/

Verona language app

- Duolingo: https://www.duolingo.com/
- Babbel: https://www.babbel.com/
- Memrise: https://www.memrise.com/

car rental apps

- Free2move: This app allows you to book and rent cars by the hour or by the day. It has a large network of vehicles in Verona, and it is relatively affordable.

- Zity: This app is another car sharing app that offers electric cars. It has a small network of vehicles in Verona, but it is growing rapidly.
- Sicily by Car: This is a traditional car rental company that has offices in Verona. It offers a wide range of vehicles to choose from, and it has competitive rates.

Suggested Itineraries

Here is a comprehensive itinerary for a 7-day solo vacation in Verona:

Day 1

- Arrive in Verona and check into your hotel.
- Take a walk around the Piazza delle Erbe and the Piazza dei Signori, two of Verona's most iconic squares.
- Visit Juliet's house and see the famous balcony where she is said to have stood and pined for Romeo.
- Have dinner at one of the many restaurants in the city center.

Day 2

- Visit the Verona Arena, a Roman amphitheater that is still used for concerts and operas today.

- Visit the Castelvecchio Museum, which houses a collection of art and artifacts from the Middle Ages to the Renaissance.

- Take a walk along the Ponte Pietra, a Roman bridge that crosses the Adige River.

- Have dinner at one of the many restaurants in the Borgo Trento neighbourhood, which is known for its traditional Veronese cuisine.

Day 3

- Visit the Basilica di San Zeno Maggiore, a beautiful Romanesque church located just outside of the city center.

- Visit the Palazzo della Ragione, a medieval palace that is now home to a museum.

- Visit the Torre dei Lamberti, a bell tower that offers stunning views of the city.

- Have dinner at one of the many restaurants in the Veronetta neighbourhood, which is known for its lively atmosphere.

Day 4

- Take a day trip to Lake Garda, one of the largest lakes in Italy.
- Visit the town of Sirmione, which is known for its beautiful beaches and its medieval castle.
- Take a boat trip on the lake and visit some of the other towns and villages that line the shore.
- Have dinner at one of the many restaurants on the lakefront.

Day 5

- Visit the Teatro Romano, a Roman theater that is still used for performances today.
- Visit the Roman Archeological Museum, which houses a collection of artifacts from the Roman period.
- Visit the Casa di Giulietta, a museum that is dedicated to the story of Romeo and Juliet.

- Have dinner at one of the many restaurants in the Borgo San Lorenzo neighbourhood, which is known for its romantic atmosphere.

Day 6

Visit the Porta Nuova, a city gate that was built in the 19th century.

- Visit the Giardino Giusti, a beautiful Renaissance garden.
- Take a cooking class and learn how to make some of Verona's traditional dishes.
- Have dinner at one of the many restaurants in the Borgo Roma neighbourhood, which is known for its modern cuisine.

Day 7

Depart from Verona.

Here is a comprehensive itinerary for a 7-day solo vacation in Verona:

Day 1

- Morning: Arrive in Verona and check into your hotel.
- Afternoon: Take a walk around the Piazza delle Erbe, the city's main square. Be sure to see the Palazzo della Ragione and the Torre dei Lamberti.
- Evening: Have dinner at one of the many family-friendly restaurants in the city center.

Day 2

- Morning: Visit the Verona Arena, a Roman amphitheater that is still used for concerts and operas today.
- Afternoon: Visit Juliet's House, the home of the fictional character Juliet from Shakespeare's Romeo and Juliet.
- Evening: Take a boat trip on the Adige River.

Day 3

● Morning: Visit the Museo Civico di Castelvecchio, an art museum housed in a medieval castle.

● Afternoon: Visit the Parco Natura Viva, a zoo located just outside of Verona.

● Evening: Have dinner at one of the many restaurants in the Borgo Trento neighbourhood, which is known for its family-friendly atmosphere.

Day 4

● Morning: Take a day trip to the Gardaland amusement park.

● Afternoon: Spend the afternoon swimming and playing in the water park at Gardaland.

● Evening: Have dinner at one of the many restaurants in the town of Peschiera del Garda, which is located near Gardaland.

Day 5

● Morning: Visit the Basilica di San Zeno Maggiore, a beautiful Romanesque church.

- Afternoon: Visit the Castel San Pietro, a castle that offers stunning views of the city.

- Evening: Have dinner at one of the many restaurants in the Piazza dei Signori, a beautiful square in the city center.

Day 6

- Morning: Visit the G.B. Cavalcaselle Museum of Verona, a museum that houses a collection of art and artifacts from the Middle Ages to the present day.

- **Afternoon:** Visit the Roman Theatre of Verona, an ancient Roman theater that is still used for performances today.

- Evening: Have dinner at one of the many restaurants in the Borgo Venezia neighbourhood, which is known for its traditional Veronese cuisine.

Day 7

- Morning: Visit the Porta Nuova railway station, a beautiful Art Nouveau building.

- Afternoon: Depart from Verona.

Essential Italian Phrases

While many in Verona speak English, a few well-chosen Italian phrases can open doors, hearts, and create lasting memories. Here are some essential expressions to enhance your experience in Verona:

Greetings and Polite Expressions:

1. Buongiorno - Good morning
2. Buonasera - Good evening
3. Buonanotte - Good night
4. Ciao - Hello / Goodbye (informal)
5. Arrivederci - Goodbye
6. Per favore - Please
7. Grazie - Thank you
8. Prego - You're welcome
9. Mi dispiace - I'm sorry
10. Scusa / Scusate - Excuse me / Excuse me (formal or plural)

Basic Communication:

11. Parla inglese? - Do you speak English?

12. Non capisco - I don't understand

13. Posso prendere...? - Can I have...?

14. Quanto costa? - How much does it cost?

15. Dove si trova...? - Where is...?

16. Mi potrebbe aiutare, per favore? - Could you help me, please?

Numbers and Directions:

17. Uno, Due, Tre... - One, Two, Three...

18. Dove? - Where?

19. Sinistra - Left

20. Destra - Right

21. Diritto - Straight ahead

22. Quant'è? - How much is it?

23. A che ora...? - At what time...?

At the Restaurant:

24. Il menu, per favore - The menu, please

25. Vorrei... - I would like...

26. L'account, per favore - The bill, please

27. Acqua - Water

28. Vino rosso / bianco - Red / White wine

29. Un caffè, per favore - A coffee, please

Emergencies:

30. Aiuto! - Help!

31. Chiamate un'ambulanza! - Call an ambulance!

32. Ho bisogno della polizia. - I need the police.

33. Sono perso / persa. - I am lost.

Getting Around:

34. Dov'è la stazione dei treni / autobus? - Where is the train / bus station?

35. Quanto dista a piedi...? - How far is it on foot...?

Remember, the key to mastering a new language is practice and confidence. Don't be afraid to make mistakes - locals will appreciate your efforts. Embrace the beauty of connecting through language in Verona.

CONCLUSION

As you near the end of your Verona journey, take a moment to reflect on the memories you've created in this enchanting city. Verona has a unique way of leaving an indelible mark on its visitors, whether through its rich history, captivating culture, or the warmth of its people.

Verona has a way of becoming a part of you. The cobblestone streets, the ancient architecture, the aroma of Italian cuisine wafting through the air - these are the experiences that stay with you long after you've left. The moments shared in Piazza delle Erbe, the echoes of your footsteps on Ponte Pietra, and the whispered wishes at Juliet's balcony - these are the threads that weave your Verona tale.

As you bid farewell to Verona, know that the city will hold a place in your heart. The memories you've collected are yours to cherish, and the spirit of Verona will be waiting to welcome you back whenever you choose to return.

Remember, this guide is more than just words on a page; it's a companion on your Verona adventure. May it have served you well in discovering the wonders of this captivating city. Until next time, arrivederci Verona!

Travel Itinerary Planner

Printed in Great Britain
by Amazon

38532910R00128